YOUR
Words
ARE Fire

YOUR
Words
ARE *Fire*

10 CULTURALLY RESPONSIVE TEACHING STRATEGIES TO SPEAK THE LANGUAGE OF BELONGING AND HELP STUDENTS LEARN, EXPRESS IDEAS, AND SOLVE PROBLEMS

HACK™
Learning
SERIES

LISSETTE JACOBSON
& MAURICE McDAVID

Cover and Interior Design by Steven Plummer
Project Management by Regina Bell
Editing by Tarah Threadgill
Copyediting by Jennifer Jas

Paperback ISBN: 978-1-956512-68-7
eBook ISBN: 978-1-956512-70-0
Hardcover ISBN: 978-1-956512-69-4

Library of Congress Cataloging-in-Publication Data is available for this title.

First Printing: May 2025

To our loving and supportive families.

And to every student who felt their language
was a barrier to their success. We see you.

TABLE OF CONTENTS

INTRODUCTION
Who Are We as Linguistic Beings?

*So, if you really want to hurt me, talk
badly about my language.*
— GLORIA ANZALDÚA, AUTHOR

THANK YOU FOR choosing to engage in this conversation around language. It is one that we hope more people will have, think about, and put into practice after reading this book. We recognize that much of the research in education focusing on Black, Indigenous, and people of color (BIPOC) and economically disadvantaged students was conducted about students like us, but not by people who look like us. As we step into this realm, we desire to bring our true selves.

We both come from families of storytellers. Our families, though hard-working and educated in many ways, did not reference research journals or articles. Instead, they presented us with incredible truths using language so powerful that we could see the stories they presented to us and understand the lessons learned by those involved. With this upbringing in mind, we begin this book with our stories. It is a way of knowing us and what brought us to this place where we are now, aware of ourselves as linguistic beings and growing in our understanding of how linguistic identity can be leveraged as a tool for education. This book is for administrators and teachers who strive to create inclusive, supportive, and transformative learning environments for every student.

Lissette's story

When you have no one to corroborate your worth, you begin to oppress yourself more than the world does. Becoming aware of my linguistic identity was painful. I was in second grade.

My linguistic consciousness began when my family moved to Waukegan, Illinois, from Chicago, the Back of the Yards community in particular. There I was with my beloved teacher, Mrs. Stewart, and my father at my parent-teacher conference. At that moment, I realized the barrier between them. My father only spoke Spanish, and my teacher only spoke English, and here I was able to speak both. I could feel my heart rate increase and my face get hot. With sweaty palms, I sank into my chair. The teacher was kind and sweet. She made no disparaging remarks, but it was her lack of acknowledgment of my bilingualism that hurt. My dad, loving and jovial, sat there smiling and nodding as many non-English-speaking immigrants do, saying yes to everything without understanding what was being said. Looking back, none of my teachers ever made any disparaging remarks about my parents, but I internalized their silence on the matter, and their silence was deafening. What should have felt like a badge of honor, my bilingualism, felt dishonorable.

For full disclosure, I don't remember translating the conversation, but what I do remember is making a conscious decision to never have school-Lissette and home-Lissette in the same room ever again. I spoke English in school and kept my nose buried in books. At home, I tried to play the role of an obedient and domestic Mexican girl. Our value as Mexican women did not come from what we knew or could accomplish. Our worth was largely measured by how well we cooked, cleaned, and took care of the men in the house. Essentially, we were to put all our needs on the back burner and live life catering to the males in the home. This was in direct opposition to what my heart truly desired.

I had dreams of going away to school and living on my own. I spent a lot of time reading at home to escape the drudgery of daily home life. This time was the beginning of my denying my identity. I knew I was different, and I didn't like how that felt. While some ethnic diversity was present, the staff did nothing to elevate the status of other languages. I would go on to hide any sort of flyers or notices that were sent home from school. I never wanted my parents to attend another parent-teacher conference or school event.

In fifth grade, I won a young authors competition. I still remember the story I wrote. It was about a young girl, Persephone, a free-spirited soul who loved school. She went from being a happy-go-lucky child to one who was dying from cancer. In the end, she survived and became a motivational speaker. It seems morbid now that I think about it. I even had her being pushed around in a wheelchair because she was too frail to move about independently. I remember some of my other friends wrote about candy shops, a princess with golden hair, and other fantastical stories. Part of me wonders what my teacher thought as she read my piece. Whatever the case, I soon went from being ecstatic about winning the competition to concerned about receiving the prize.

I did not tell my family because I knew I would have to spend the entire time translating. We did not attend the award ceremony.

Language has always been a major factor in my life. I am the fourth of five children, and my siblings were in bilingual classrooms between kindergarten and third grade. At this time, bilingual education was seen as remedial, and the goal was to get you to speak English as quickly as possible and then exit you to monolingual English classes. An analogy often used is "throwing you in the water to get you to swim" or "pushing you off a bridge and expecting you to fly." The reality was that this model of bilingual education clipped students' wings and prevented them from soaring.

Much of my academic career was characterized by a dual identity. I applied myself to my work, but I also dabbled with trouble. I was in honors classes during high school but preferred not to hang out with the kids in my classes. They were not what my peer group considered "cool," and they were primarily White. I had little in common with them. They loved quoting *Seinfeld*, while I would rather quote the lyrics to my favorite hip-hop song.

I would get praised at school for my love of reading and writing. But at home, my parents would call me lazy for opting to read or write instead of helping my mother with chores around the house. This situation would lead to full-blown arguments. I once told my mom she knew nothing when she criticized me for reading so much. I could tell I had hurt her feelings, and that made me feel guilty. Again, school-Lissette and home-Lissette had to exist separately. It was exhausting.

Once, I got into a fist fight at school and was suspended for three days. Girls used to bully me over trivial things. I eventually got so fed up with it that when this girl bumped into me, I punched her in the face. I had to defend myself or risk being bullied throughout the remainder of the year. It was only October. When the school office called my home, my sister answered. She pretended to be my mom because my mother does not speak English. This "pretend parent" role was one my oldest sister often assumed for her siblings. At the time, I remember feeling like this was to my advantage. My parents never found out about the suspension. Eventually, in adulthood, I realized how terrible it was that my parents had not been getting communication about their children in the language they speak, and how much that isolated me in school.

My senior year was a blur. I had surrendered to the idea that I would attend community college and not a four-year school like many of my classmates. None of my siblings attended college, and my parents were okay with them finishing high school and immediately transitioning to working full time. I had bigger dreams. My father, being the traditional Mexican man that he is, struggled with the idea that I would be living outside of the home and unmarried. He even called me indecent for having such aspirations.

My high school guidance counselor, Mr. Wilts, was perplexed by this. He asked what my future goals were, and I expressed that I wanted to teach more than anything. He said I was too bright *not* to go to college. Mr. Wilts feared that I would never complete a degree if I wanted to go to community college because he saw this happen to many other graduates from my high school. He asked if he could talk to my parents to see if he could change their minds. I told him they did not speak English, and I walked out of his office.

Mr. Wilts was persistent; he would find me during the passing periods and talk to me. I eventually devised a plan to graduate early so I could work full time to save up money for school. Mr. Wilts told me that he agreed with me graduating early but also found a way to potentially get $30,000 for college if I went to a four-year school, alleviating my other pressing concern about attending college. The Golden Apple Foundation recruits one hundred high school seniors from across the state to help prepare them to be excellent teachers. We did not have a home computer that worked well. It would shut off sporadically, and I had to constantly save my work, which slowed me down drastically.

In hindsight, the selection process was rigorous, especially for someone like me who did not have the cultural or social capital to navigate the educational system. Again, my parents could not fully comprehend what I was doing because of the language difference, plus I desired to keep them away from it all. They did not choose this; I chose for them. These were additional barriers that others did not have to face.

My parents eventually conceded to my requests to go away to school. After doing all the prep work on my own—the applications, the FAFSA, the registration, the scholarships—they really had no choice. Eight essays, three letters of recommendation, and two interviews later, I was selected as a Golden Apple Scholar. This scholarship changed the trajectory of my life forever.

I adore my parents, and they have done the best they could with the little they had. While I never thought of myself as someone who was oppressed because of my race, I certainly felt linguistically oppressed. I struggled unnecessarily because of the limited linguistic resources available in schools. If more language support had been in place, I believe my parents would have been more involved in my academics. Once, when I was visiting my parents, my dad shared how intimidating it was for him to go to school functions. I had never considered this before. While I was so caught up in my embarrassment, my struggles to get as far as I had, I assumed my dad was content with his obliviousness. My heart now breaks for him.

As an educator, I often hear teachers' lounge conversations. Assumptions about parents not caring about their child's education upset me most. I know this could not be further from the truth. Maybe there are other Lissettes like me, keeping their parents away.

Maurice's story

Place has always been important to me. How I view my identity has always been connected to the place I call home. Whether in the small city where I grew up or the small town where I attended college, I have taken pride in the location. I wore the colors of my high school and college with pride. The impact of my locations has been intense. The Chicago Bears are the football team I root for. Corn is my favorite vegetable. I love the colors black and orange (my high school colors).

In more pronounced ways, my hometown has impacted far more significant parts of my identity. It was in my hometown that I met my wife who was my high school sweetheart. It was there that I became a Christian and received my call to ministry at the same church I still attend. It was in that town where I became a father, an educator, an administrator, and an author.

Place, as it relates to our discussion in this book, caused me to see that language is indeed a part of our identity. It is intriguing for me because the overwhelming majority of students in the school buildings I attended as a child spoke English. Not only did they speak English, but they spoke middle-class, Midwestern English. The elementary school I first attended was predominantly White. There were four Black students, including me, and two Latino students. Neither of the Latino students spoke Spanish at home, and all the students were born and raised in DeKalb, Illinois. There were no accents to speak of. In my second-grade classroom, although some of us looked different, we all sounded the same.

Third grade changed that experience for me. In the spring of my second-grade year, my mother, my brothers, and I moved to another part of DeKalb. In doing so, I transferred from my previous school to a school with a far different student population. At that time, many people were moving into DeKalb from Chicago. Many of these people were Black and brought with them an experience far different from what DeKalb had been before their arrival—a small community in the middle of a farming county.

Along with their experiences, these new community members and classmates brought their language. They brought the language of the hip-hop movement of the late 1990s. They brought a language rooted in the Great Migration of the early to mid-twentieth century. They brought with them an urban swagger and adaptability that was present in their speech. And in that moment, I was introduced to the idea of "talking Black."

The questions initially came from my Black classmates. "Why do you talk like that?" they would ask me. "That," of course, was what some would later define as "talking White." It was the diction and enunciation that I was used to, having grown up in DeKalb. My Black peers noted that I did not sound like many of them, though I looked like them. It did not take long for the vocabulary of my friends to begin to be part of my daily use. In this way, even at an early age, the linguistics of place impacted how I presented myself.

Early on, I learned the popular social phrases and used them regularly in my neighborhood, which was increasingly Black. I did not, however, integrate the new language into my classroom communication. I don't know that it was intentional or that I even understood at the time how language was used to determine the value of people. Whatever it was, I maintained the status quo in my elementary school experience. In the neighborhood, though, I began to use expressions like *calling cobs* to protect my snacks from my friends or saying *that's tight* to describe something cool. I felt a part of the neighborhood. I felt I had a people and that even though we were from different places, we were connected through our language. It was the beginning of forming my linguistic identity, yet I was not yet aware of it.

Middle school, which in our school system was organized with fifth and sixth grades in one building and seventh and eighth in another, would subtly impact my linguistic development. At school, I hung out with friends from my early elementary years, but in the neighborhood, I continued to work to fit in linguistically. Academically, I was placed in advanced classes, which, unfortunately, left me as the only Black person in class for much of my day. Also, I played football on a team with a level of diversity that did not match the school's, and all of these factors played a role in my linguistic identity development.

As I prepared to transition out of middle school, my older brother, who was five and a half years my senior, attempted to prepare me for high school. He told me two things. First, he said my football team would not win games in high school. I argued, exclaiming that we had been conference champs. The second thing he told me was that my White friends were going to take note of the fact that I was Black, and it was going to make a difference. We went zero-to-nine in our freshman year as a football team. And, unfortunately, his other prophecy also came to pass.

It started with subtle race-based jokes, but it quickly escalated into declarations of my Whiteness because of my academic success and, of course, the way I spoke. In my sophomore and junior years, two events brought me face-to-face with my linguistic identity. One event was acted out by the Black students at the school, and the other was enacted by the White students at our building.

My sophomore year included school events that led to the founding of a Black Student Union, and we had to fight through an incredible pushback to get it established. In the fall, a poster on one of the bulletin boards inviting students to try out for the cheerleading team was defaced. A student had written on the poster, "No N*ggers Allowed!" A few months later, in another hallway and on another poster that read, "Why can't we all get along," someone responded, "Because you're all n*ggers." In January of that school year, the Black students at the high school began to meet with local Black leaders and formulate the idea of a BSU. When the news spread, there was pushback from White students, staff, and community members. We had to go to the school board for the final decision.

As we collaborated in our meetings, we knew someone would have to speak before the board. When I was asked to speak and was told that my "diction" would be well received by the majority-White school board, I saw that language was indeed part of my identity that could be used to access power. Several other students and I spoke before that board and successfully brought a BSU to the school. It was not, however, the end of challenges around this topic.

In my junior year, a newspaper was named after the neighborhood where I lived. This newspaper truly represented the ingenuity of teenagers in an age before the existence of a computing device in every home. The paper featured stories about the neighborhood, the goings-on of our school, and a section called "Oreos." If you are unfamiliar with this term, it is meant to be derogatory in that it describes a person who, though appearing Black, is really "White" on the inside. This section of the paper, produced by my Black peers from my neighborhood, listed Black students who were "Oreos" and gave the reason why.

I was incredibly grateful that my name was not listed there, but I cringed when I saw the names, including one of my friends. The paper said that even though he was Black, he talked "White." This student came from a home in which both of his parents were professors. They had immigrated to the United

States from Kenya, stopping in England and then Maryland before landing in Illinois. It was amazing. He was someone with roots in Africa that were clearly visible, but his language separated him from his peers, whose families had been in the US for generations.

I determined right then that, right or wrong, I would never let that happen to me. I would never allow my identity to be questioned because of the way I speak. I went on to craft an intentional way of speaking for each environment I was in. Only recently have I felt comfortable integrating my home language and my school language. For me, this process was helped by learning a language other than English. Studying abroad in Spain and then working with Spanish-speaking students and families gave me the confidence to challenge the linguistic norms that otherwise hold us in check and leave us feeling as though we can only speak one way if we are to be successful.

Where do we go from here?

We shared our personal stories that have brought us to this point in our journey. Through our personal experience and the current research, we endeavor to present to you that there is no one language of success. Instead, all students have a language, and that language is an entry point. It is part of who each student is. We put forward the idea that language is so tightly tied with identity that any attempt to degrade the language a person is speaking will almost always be seen as a degradation of the person. Language is culture. Language is history. Language is identity. So then, as we attempt to integrate any responsive pedagogy (including culturally or historically responsive), we must see that language plays a major role.

We posit three critical points on which this book is based:

1. Language and identity are tied together. Build them both to see the most success in building people who identify as lifelong learners.

2. Language is an incredible foundation to build on as you work with students across every content area.

3. The "standard" version of a language, as it is defined in this moment, cannot be the end-all be-all because language is fluid and continuously changing. Being adaptable in your language is the key to every future-oriented position in the workforce.

Again, we thank you for joining us on this journey as we discuss how we may leverage non-standard language as a tool in the educational process.

HACK
1

LEARN LINGUISTICS 101
Understand How Language Evolves

The English language is truly productive. New words can be created with relative ease. Some see this as characteristic of vigor and vitality; others see it as signs of mind rot or lower standards in schools.
— LARRY ANDREWS, AUTHOR

THE PROBLEM: EDUCATORS OFTEN DON'T UNDERSTAND THEIR LANGUAGE BIAS

EDUCATORS TYPICALLY RECEIVE minimal formal training on how language works or the fundamentals of linguistics, despite language's critical role in all aspects of teaching and learning. Understanding how language develops, how students acquire multiple languages, and how linguistic diversity shapes learning is essential for effective instruction. Without this foundational knowledge, many educators may struggle to fully support language learners, missing key opportunities to enhance comprehension, communication, and academic success. Equipping educators with a deeper understanding of linguistics empowers them to better meet the needs of all students.

People are biased about language. Bias can develop at an early age, often through direct and indirect instruction. I was conversing with my wife in Spanish, as we did on purpose when we did not want our children to know what we were saying. I vividly remember my youngest daughter telling me, as seriously as possible, "Speak normal!" She did not ask me to speak English but instead asked me to speak in a way that her bias presented as normal. This, of course, came from the only kind of direct instruction she had received up to that point. The indirect instruction she had received was that English is the *norm* and all other languages are *foreign*.

Our parents and our home lives are not the only factors that inform our bias. Because humans mainly classify information based on the schema, the "mental maps" they have gained through life experiences, many factors impact bias. Mental maps are the internal representations or frameworks people create to organize and interpret the world around them. These "maps" are formed through experiences, cultural influences, and knowledge, helping individuals categorize new information, make decisions, and respond to situations based on prior understanding. Mental maps can be helpful to process information quickly, but they can also lead to bias when they oversimplify or reinforce stereotypes.

Examples of mental maps:

1. **Cultural stereotypes:** A person may develop a mental map associating certain professions (e.g., doctors or engineers) with specific genders or ethnic groups based on societal influences. This mental map

can shape their expectations and assumptions about who belongs in those roles.

2. **Neighborhood safety perception:** Someone who grew up in a suburban area might have a mental map that associates cities with being dangerous, even if they have never personally experienced crime in an urban setting. This mental map influences how they perceive and navigate new environments.

The culture of the geographic location where a person is raised is key. Also significant is the amount and type of media someone consumes. The news, for example, offers images of what an immigrant without legal status looks like, and an image forms in our schema. The media's use of images leads us to believe that an overwhelming majority of immigrants in the country without authorization are from Mexico. This is accurate, but the part of the story that is rarely told is the 1.7 million people from Asia who are in the US with the same immigration status. As a result, people's biases about immigrants from Asia may differ from their biases about those from Central and South America.

Bias, while occurring naturally in people, can be detrimental, even dangerous, when not dealt with properly. Generally, in diversity, equity, and inclusion work, bias is talked about in two forms, explicit and implicit, with one having a greater impact in the education world. Explicit bias is a form of bias that is clear and visible. The person holding explicit bias is aware of it and acts on it. Implicit bias, on the other hand, differs in that an educator holding implicit bias may not be aware of it. It is represented by the set of ideas that one simply considers as "normal." A person's biases, thoughts, and opinions impact the person's interactions with others. We make decisions based on biases we may hold about the way a student dresses, acts, and speaks.

Linguistic bias

Linguistic bias is a bias against people who speak another language or dialect, or a bias toward bilingual speakers. In education, this often results in an inaccurate assessment of children from linguistic backgrounds other than Standard American English (SAE). Many educators acknowledge that students of color are overrepresented in special education programs when, in fact, they are language learners like all of us.

Standard American English is a form of English that's generally used in professional communication in the United States and taught in American schools. It is important to note that SAE is a real institutional construct that begets power. A small group of people determines the rules of spoken and written SAE, meaning most people who speak English are not responsible for developing these norms and nuances. If sampled daily, we would find that most people break these rules regularly. Furthermore, because the English language is dynamic, mastering it is not a one-time task. We must constantly adjust, adapt, and revise what we have learned.

Standard American English is not inherently more beautiful, appropriate, or better. People with social power can impose this variety of the English language on the rest of us. They can make SAE more prestigious. Since social power is desired by many, SAE is often seen as a conduit of upward mobility. Linguistic bias in favor of SAE by the education system necessitates that other forms of English be thought of as less than.

THE HACK: LEARN LINGUISTICS 101

Language is a fundamental component of communication and understanding our world. With knowledge and appreciation of linguistics, we gain insight into different cultural perspectives and bridge misunderstandings between people and societies.

In school settings, students must learn about language dynamics in order to be successful communicators. It also benefits their learning because it enables them to conduct a contrastive analysis between their home language and the language spoken in school. When students study linguistics, they develop more effective communication skills that promote respectful discourse and collaboration across diverse groups.

Various professionals study linguistics, including linguists, educators, psychologists, sociologists, and anthropologists. In an education context, linguistics is often studied by language acquisition specialists, speech-language pathologists, curriculum designers, and teachers who work with multilingual learners or students with language-based learning needs. Linguistics provides students with an appreciation for the complexity of languages and an understanding of how languages shape our culture and society. This appreciation elevates the status of languages other than Standard American English and deepens students' understanding of other languages and dialects.

BY LEARNING ABOUT LINGUISTIC DYNAMICS, STUDENTS BECOME BETTER PREPARED FOR GLOBAL INTERACTIONS IN AN INCREASINGLY INTERCONNECTED WORLD.

Linguistics also helps people understand the cognitive processes that occur when we think and communicate with one another, from the production of speech sounds to the construction of meaningful sentences. Furthermore, by studying linguistics in school settings, students learn how language works on a larger scale throughout society, such as how language creates social hierarchies and contributes to social change. The following list of "other" types of English includes potential ideas for conversation-starters to share with students as young as kindergarten in a way that is appropriate to their age or grade level. While schools don't typically offer a specific curriculum for the study of linguistics, discussing other languages and dialects while teaching English is a great way to integrate linguistics into the classroom.

"Other" English

- **AAVE:** In the academic world, the vernacular of English spoken by Black people is often referred to as African American Vernacular English (AAVE), but you may also hear laypeople refer to it as Ebonics. African American Vernacular English is a dialect of English spoken by many Black Americans across the United States, regardless of socioeconomic status or education. This vernacular, however, has historically been identified with a lack of education or even intelligence. Consider the minstrel shows that began in the 1830s, in which White actors would not only paint their faces black but also change the way they spoke, exaggerating the language to connect it with a lack of intelligence.

  AAVE is not English with mistakes. Two prominent hypotheses describe how AAVE came to be. On the one hand, there is what's known as the Anglicist Hypothesis, which proposes that enslaved African people on Southern plantations acquired English from their British owners. On the other hand, the Creolist Hypothesis proposes that AAVE originated from a Creole spoken on Southern plantations before the Civil War.

  Creole is a whole language that developed from pidgin, a grammatically simplified language created between two groups who need to communicate but do not share a common language. Linguists of this view say AAVE arose from a Creole in West Africa. Thus, enslaved people already spoke the language before coming to the US. Regardless of the hypothesis you align to, the fact is that African American Vernacular English is widely spoken by countless students in our schools, and many are subjected to prejudice and biases that negatively impact their schooling experience.

- **Chicano English:** Chicano English, or ChE, is a dialect spoken primarily by Mexican Americans, particularly those in California and the Southwest. Much like AAVE, it is not beginner English or watered-down Spanish. I have heard many educators ask, "Why do many Mexican Americans struggle to speak proper English when they were born in the United States?" Others have heard students speak Chicano English and are astounded by the fact that these students do not speak Spanish. Many will hear the accent and assume that the students' native language is Spanish. Despite people's mistaken impressions, these Mexican American speakers have learned English natively and fluently, like most children growing up in the US. They just happened to have learned a variety of English indicative of contact with the Spanish language. It would be a mistake to characterize Chicano English as "learner English" with imperfections and non-native lingo. ChE is a fully formed dialect, linguistically and structurally equivalent to other dialects of English, much like the "Valley Girl" style that characterizes Anglo girls in California.

- **Slang:** If you conduct an internet search of the word "slang," you will find various definitions. For the sake of this text, we will use the following definition for slang. Slang is speech and writing characterized by vulgar and socially taboo vocabulary and idiomatic expressions.

Slang, by recent accounts, has been associated with African American culture, but did you know that words we may consider innocent and common, such as *piano*, *zoo*, and *bus*, were once considered slang terms? The "correct" terms are pianoforte, zoological garden, and omnibus. While piano, zoo, and bus are now considered a part of Standard American English, this shows how dynamic and versatile English truly is.

IT'S ESSENTIAL FOR STUDENTS TO UNDERSTAND THE IMPACT OF TECHNOLOGY ON LANGUAGE, AS IT DIRECTLY INFLUENCES HOW WE COMMUNICATE IN THE DIGITAL AGE.

This problem of creating a linguistic hierarchy does not exist only in English. In many Spanish/English dual language classrooms, a hierarchy also exists regarding Spanish. A student from Mexico may consider his Spanish to be superior to the Spanish spoken in Honduras. Even within Mexico, city Spanish may be regarded as better than country Spanish. Whether English, Spanish, or another language altogether, these linguistic biases can negatively impact how we interact with our students and how they interact with one another. By adopting a linguistic perspective of languages, we can begin to diminish the linguistic bias in many institutions, particularly schools. Let's look at language and its versatility as vigor and vitality, not the lowering of standards.

All these aspects make it clear why it's essential to learn about linguistics in school settings to provide a better understanding of communication systems between people and offer insights into how language operates in different contexts. By learning about linguistic dynamics, students become better prepared for global interactions in an increasingly interconnected world.

WHAT 𝒴𝒪𝒰 CAN DO TOMORROW

The ideas that follow are relatively simple but can yield immense positive results. While they may require self-awareness and reflection, you can leverage them to improve student outcomes. These concepts center linguistics to develop language-rich environments. The final idea is a checklist you can access on the Resources tab of our website, blackbrownbilingue.com.

- **Display text and images with different languages and dialects throughout your class or school.** This first step may seem like a no-brainer, but you will be surprised how infrequently this occurs in schools. Even if your school and community do not necessarily have linguistic diversity, our world has become more interconnected, and diversity will grow as the technological landscape keeps evolving. Displaying text and images with different languages and dialects on classroom walls and bulletin boards gives students the exposure they need to be global citizens. Display these images in high-traffic spaces like main entryways, bathrooms, and hallways. Our brains are wired for visual processing. We can process images with small phrases far more quickly than we can process written text only.

  For example, it is common to see posters in classrooms with the quote attributed to Mahatma Gandhi, "Be the change you wish to see in the world." A curious fact about this quote is that while it has been printed in English countless times, the language in which it was originally uttered was Gujarati. We propose including the quote in its original language alongside the English translation to broaden students' views of the world around them.

- **Designate part of your classroom for a metalinguistic focus.** Metalinguistic cognition is one type of metacognition in which students develop their ability to think about language objectively, reflect on it, and analyze it. Simply put, it is the ability to analyze your own thinking about language. To learn more about this topic, see our blog post, "Metalinguistic Awareness in Every Classroom" available on our website. Incorporating language into your practice as an educator is another simple step. Find a space in your classroom where you can highlight various language complexities to raise students' linguistic awareness.

    For example, children are enormously interested in wordplay and riddles. They are fun and help children make discoveries about language that have been shown to improve their reading comprehension. Understanding that words and sentences can have multiple meanings improves comprehension by allowing readers to think flexibly about the appropriate meaning. Did you know that the thousand most commonly used words in the English language are multiply ambiguous? Not only can the words in a sentence be ambiguous and have multiple meanings, but syntax also plays a role in comprehension. Take, for instance, the sentence, "The bat flew into the batting cage." It can mean both the animal and the baseball bat.

- **Explicitly consider the impact of technology on language.** The advent of technology has significantly accelerated the evolution of language, bringing about new dynamics in communication. Digital platforms, primarily social media and messaging apps, have fostered the emergence of new words, phrases, and ways of expressing ideas. A notable example is the use of emojis, which have virtually formed a new sub-language, transcending linguistic barriers and offering a universal way of conveying emotions and ideas. Similarly, acronyms such as "lol," "brb," and "ttyl" have gained widespread usage, illustrating how technology influences the development of linguistic shortcuts. Moreover, autocorrect and predictive text features have also affected spelling and grammar, sometimes generating new forms of words or phrases. It's essential for students to understand the impact of technology on language, as it directly influences how we communicate in the digital age. By incorporating this aspect into teaching, educators can better prepare students for a world where language continues to evolve swiftly and unpredictably.

- **Share how new words have been made.** Teachers can also introduce students to the concept of language borrowing and how it contributes to language evolution. Many languages have borrowed words from other languages through trade or cultural interactions. This knowledge can help students understand that language is not static but is constantly influenced by external factors. Examples of borrowed words include:

- ▸ alcohol (Arabic)
- ▸ boss (Dutch)
- ▸ avocado, coyote (Nahuatl)
- ▸ croissant (French)
- ▸ pretzel (German)
- ▸ yogurt (Turkish)
- ▸ zebra (Bantu)

• **Read articles about linguistics in a school setting.** Linguistics is the scientific study of language and its structure, including the study of grammar, syntax, phonetics, semantics, and pragmatics. It also covers aspects such as historical evolution and the societal impact of languages. Teachers may wonder why it is important to read articles about linguistics in school. The following points shed light on the significance of this practice:

- ▸ *Enhancing teaching skills:* One main reason teachers should read articles on linguistics is to enhance their teaching skills. By understanding the complex nature of language and its various components, teachers can improve their ability to teach grammar, syntax, and other linguistic concepts effectively. This skill can help them develop more engaging and interactive lessons for their students, thus ensuring better learning outcomes. Additionally, reading linguistics articles introduces teachers to new and innovative teaching methodologies they may not have known before.

▸ *Keeping up with language evolution:* Language is constantly evolving, and reading articles about linguistics allows teachers to keep track of how languages are changing over time and the factors contributing to these changes. This practice can help them better understand their students' use of language and address any challenges they face in learning or in using a particular language.

Additionally, awareness of linguistic developments can help teachers incorporate more relevant and current examples into their lessons. Great places to find articles about linguistics include Kids Britannica or the website study.com. Superlinguo also provides a recommended list of children's books about linguistics.

▸ *Examine your biases pertaining to language:* Our website, blackbrownbilingue.com, offers the resource "Language Bias in the Classroom: A Checklist." It is a collection of questions based on research related to bias and applied specifically to language. Please consider using this resource as a tool to help you prepare to be a culturally responsive and sustaining educator as you reflect on language's powerful role in student success. It is a great way to begin a personal reflection on how you think about and interact with language that is alike and different from yours and the people who speak it.

A BLUEPRINT FOR FULL IMPLEMENTATION

The integration of language within a school is a significant thread that requires the careful weaving of consensus among all stakeholders. The school board must serve as guardians of this process and as thought partners to educators, analyzing data to identify the needs and successes of current initiatives. Building consensus isn't just a procedural step; it's the foundational stone to improve student outcomes. The suggestions range from actions you can take individually to those that will help you bring others on board.

STEP 1: Seek thought partners.

One way for teachers to educate themselves about linguistics is to seek thought partners in their schools or educational communities. Thought partners collaborate to exchange ideas, provide feedback, and challenge thinking to deepen understanding and generate innovative solutions. They can be other teachers, administrators, or linguistics experts. By engaging in discussions and exchanging ideas with these individuals, teachers can gain valuable insights and knowledge about linguistic concepts and how to apply them in school settings. In school settings, the examples focus heavily on applied linguistics, particularly in areas related to:

- **Language acquisition:** Understand how students learn a first or additional language, including the stages of language development and factors that influence language learning.

- **Sociolinguistics:** Explore how students' cultural and linguistic backgrounds impact their language use, identity, and academic experiences.

- **Language variation and dialects:** Recognize and respect linguistic diversity, including dialectal variations and how they influence students' learning experiences.

- **Bilingual and multilingual education:** Develop instructional strategies and curricula that support language learners, such as dual language programs and language bridging.

- **Linguistic equity:** Address biases and inequities related to language use, such as dialect discrimination or assumptions about students based on their language proficiency.

Thought partners can also help teachers stay updated on the latest research and advancements in linguistics.

STEP 2: Learn all you can.

Teachers can attend workshops and training sessions specifically focused on linguistics in education. These opportunities may be offered by educational institutions, professional organizations, or linguistic experts. By participating in these events, teachers can learn about various linguistic theories and their practical applications in the classroom. Moreover, they can network with other educators with similar interests and goals, leading to a more collaborative learning experience. Webinars are another good option because they offer flexible, cost-effective professional development opportunities that can be accessed from anywhere. They allow teachers to engage with experts, stay current on educational trends, and gain valuable knowledge without the time and financial constraints of travel. Additionally, many webinars are recorded, allowing educators to learn at their own pace.

For teachers who want to delve deeper into linguistics, pursuing further education may be a viable option. Options include enrolling in college courses or online programs that offer specialized training in linguistics and its applications in education. Many universities also offer graduate programs focused on language teaching and learning, providing educators with advanced knowledge and skills to enhance their teaching practices. Teachers should also research if their county will pay for enrolling in these classes, especially if the courses can help teachers work toward their recertification requirements.

STEP 3: Get your leaders on board.

One key way to promote multilingualism in schools is to get leaders on board. School leaders significantly influence a school's culture and policies, making their support crucial in creating an inclusive environment for all languages. Teacher leaders can also help do the heavy lifting to promote this understanding. Here are a few strategies for teachers to engage school leaders in elevating all languages:

- **Educate teachers on the benefits of multilingualism.** School leaders are often tasked with instructional leadership, a considerable undertaking, and may not be aware of how they can leverage the promotion of all languages to improve student performance. As supporters of linguistic awareness, we are responsible for educating school stakeholders about the numerous benefits of being multilingual, such as improving cognitive skills, enhancing cultural understanding, and increasing global opportunities. This knowledge will help educators understand why it is important to elevate all languages in our schools.

- **Share success stories.** A powerful way to inspire school leaders is to share the success stories of students who excelled academically and personally due to their multilingualism. These real-life examples can be a compelling reminder of the impact that promoting all languages can have on students.

- **Involve educators in language events.** Organizing language events within the school can be a great way to showcase the diversity and value of different languages. As teachers, we can involve school leaders by inviting them to attend or participate in these events as special guests. This experience will give teachers a firsthand look at how promoting all languages can foster a sense of belonging and inclusivity in our school community. Examples of language events include:

  - ▶ *Multilingual storytelling night:* Families and students are invited to share stories in their home languages, followed by English translations or summaries. This event celebrates linguistic diversity and fosters a sense of community by highlighting various cultural narratives.

> ▶ *Language fair:* Students create presentations, displays, and performances showcasing the different languages spoken at school. The fair may include language booths, cultural artifacts, traditional music, and food samples, helping peers learn about various linguistic backgrounds.

> ▶ *Poetry slam or spoken word event:* Students perform original poems or spoken word pieces in different languages, allowing them to express their identity, creativity, and emotions through language. This event helps promote language appreciation and confidence in multilingual expression.

> ▶ *World language week:* This schoolwide celebration includes daily activities focused on learning phrases in different languages, inviting guest speakers, and integrating language-related activities into classroom instruction.

> ▶ *Language recognition ceremony:* This event honors multilingual students, awarding them certificates for their proficiency in multiple languages or for completing bilingual education programs.

- **Collaborate on language policies.** School leaders play key roles in setting policies and guidelines. Teachers can collaborate with them to create or revise existing policies that promote all languages. This effort could include implementing language classes in younger grades and outside of world language requirements in high school, encouraging bilingualism, and providing resources for students from non-English-speaking backgrounds. Moreover, policies can include implications for language in the classroom. For example, students can be encouraged to use their home languages when brainstorming, drafting, or discussing ideas. Other examples include:

- ▶ The school will provide translated materials and interpretation services to communicate clearly with families.
- ▶ Teachers will receive professional development on strategies for incorporating students' home languages in classroom instruction.
- ▶ By involving school leaders in the process, they are more likely to support and champion these policies.

- **Show them the bigger picture.** In today's globalized world, being multilingual is not just a personal benefit but also a necessity for success. As educators, we can help school leaders understand that by promoting all languages in our schools, we are preparing our students to be successful global citizens who thrive in diverse environments. This shift in perspective can help school leaders see the importance of elevating all languages.

STEP 4: Dig into data.

People aren't always swayed by anecdotal accounts or stories; some individuals will only be moved by evidence in the form of concrete numbers. Data can provide valuable insights into how students perform in different areas, including language proficiency. If you work explicitly with students who are learning English as a second language, you may know that WIDA (World-Class Instructional Design and Assessment) is an organization that provides excellent language acquisition assessments. More generally, programs such as NWEA MAP and iReady provide great data regarding students' English proficiency.

By gathering and analyzing data, schools can identify trends and patterns in student achievement and potential barriers to success. Students may have developed skills in one language and types of knowledge in another language. Often, we see that monolingual peers view students as discrepant because their full linguistic repertoire has not been considered. Educators can use this information to inform decisions around language policies and support strategies for students.

Data analysis also allows schools to track individual students' progress and specific subgroups within the student population. By monitoring and analyzing data regularly, schools can quickly identify areas where intervention is necessary and make informed decisions to improve student outcomes.

Furthermore, data analysis can reveal disparities in student achievement among different language groups. You can use this information to address any inequities and ensure that all students have equal opportunities to succeed. Schools can also use data to identify successful practices and strategies by high-performing language groups and implement them more widely. This practice promotes equity and allows for continuous improvement in language policies and support systems.

Quick tip: Check with your school-based or county testing coordinators or your special education department to see what resources they already have that you might tailor for this use.

STEP 5: Develop school improvement goals around language.

By developing school improvement goals around language, schools send a powerful message to students, parents, and the broader community that language matters. It demonstrates a commitment to fostering a learning environment where all students can succeed regardless of their linguistic background. It also acknowledges and values the diverse languages and cultures within the school community, promoting inclusion and belonging among students.

When developing language improvement goals, consider the specific needs and challenges the student population faces, which may include English language learners, students with learning disabilities, or those from marginalized communities. By identifying the unique needs, schools can create targeted goals that address language development for all students.

Here are examples of language improvement goals that schools can set:

- Increase the number of students who achieve proficiency in English as a second language.

- Provide targeted language support for students with learning disabilities to improve their reading and writing skills. For example, incorporate both English language development (ELD) and home language proficiency goals into the Individualized Education Plan (IEP) to support bilingual growth alongside academic progress.

- Promote cultural competency and understanding among students by incorporating diverse literature and activities into the curriculum. Diverse literature refers to texts that authentically represent the identities, cultures, and experiences of underrepresented groups. It fosters inclusivity, promotes empathy, and helps students see themselves and others in the stories they read.

- Encourage bilingualism and biliteracy among students by offering language immersion programs for those learning another language or language courses for heritage speakers to support students who are still developing their English.

- Create a welcoming and inclusive school environment by celebrating the diversity of languages and cultures within the school community.

STEP 6: Work linguistic lessons into your classroom.

One way to explicitly teach students about language evolution is by introducing them to the concept of language families. Languages are often grouped into families based on common origins and similarities in grammar and vocabulary. By exploring different language families, students can see how languages have evolved and how they are interconnected. This knowledge can also help them understand the roots of certain words and how they have been adapted and borrowed into different languages.

The Indo-European family of languages is a prevalent example. It includes English, Spanish, German, Russian, and Hindi, among others. These languages have a common ancestral language known as Proto-Indo-European, which was spoken thousands of years ago. Another example is the Sino-Tibetan language family, consisting of Chinese, Burmese, and many other languages spoken in East Asia. These examples demonstrate how languages within the same family share common characteristics and structures, indicating a shared history and evolution.

Another essential aspect to cover is the influence of historical events on language evolution. For example, major historical events such as colonization and migration have significantly impacted language development. By discussing these events and their effects, students can gain a deeper understanding of why certain languages have evolved in certain ways and how they continue to change.

OVERCOMING PUSHBACK

Overcoming pushback in the realm of language and education is no small feat, especially when the objective of language education is to enhance student learning through the proficient use of academic English in the US classroom. The challenge rests with the common misconception that focusing exclusively on academic English might supplant the rich diversity of other languages and dialects in the learning environment. Additionally, it is important to understand the reasons behind a teacher's refusal to incorporate different languages and dialects.

Many teachers have not received training or education about teaching students from diverse linguistic backgrounds. However, triumph is possible through a dedicated approach that emphasizes the value of learning academic English as a skill set integral to academic success and future opportunities, while respecting and encouraging the multilingual tapestry that each student brings into the classroom. Here are a few common concerns about this Hack and how to address them.

Students should focus on learning academic English, as other languages or dialects hinder their progress. Responding to teachers who believe students should only prioritize academic English can be challenging. However, have open and respectful communication with your colleagues. You can explain the benefits of incorporating a student's native language or dialect in their learning, as it enhances their overall language skills and promotes a sense of belonging and cultural sensitivity in the classroom.

Another way to address this concern is by providing evidence-based research that supports the notion of multilingual education. Studies have shown that students who are bilingual or multilingual have higher cognitive flexibility, critical thinking skills, and academic success. Presenting the research supports the idea that learning academic English does not mean neglecting other languages or dialects; instead, it can enhance a student's overall language development.

It is also important to remind teachers during faculty meetings, professional learning communities (PLCs), and other communication opportunities that by incorporating a student's native language or dialect, they promote inclusivity and create a more dynamic and engaging learning environment for all students. Encouraging cultural exchange and understanding can foster empathy and respect among students, preparing them to be global citizens in a diverse world. From small actions such as learning greetings in multiple languages to more involved steps such as asking students to consider the impact of language on a particular event in history or a text, educators must proceed with intentionality.

My students already speak academic English. Today's society values diversity and inclusivity, especially in educational and work settings. Teachers need to recognize and incorporate languages and dialects other than Standard English to prepare students for a global society. You can also provide evidence or research that supports this practice. Avoid accusing administrators and staff of refusing to promote language learning and belonging, as this may lead to a defensive response. Instead, focus on finding common ground and working toward a solution together.

All teachers are language teachers because language is central to learning in every subject. Whether students are learning math, science, social studies, or art, they must understand and use the specific academic language required to engage with the content. Academic English, with its specialized vocabulary, sentence structures, and discourse patterns, presents a challenge for students, making language development an ongoing process across all disciplines.

Whether you are a building administrator or a teacher, offering support and resources is an effective way to encourage other educators to incorporate different languages and dialects in their teaching. You can provide them with teaching materials or strategies and even offer to co-teach a lesson. Remind the teacher that incorporating different languages and dialects does not mean sacrificing the English language but enhancing it by promoting linguistic diversity.

I will not understand my students if we encourage another spoken language. Some teachers may express concern about promoting the use of multiple spoken languages in the classroom, stating that they only speak one language and will not be able to understand their students. Teachers may fear that promoting other languages and dialects will lead to students disrespecting staff or other students without their knowledge. While this may seem like a valid concern, remember that promoting multilingualism can benefit teachers and their students. One approach could be to educate teachers about how to effectively teach and communicate with their students, including by providing resources such as translation tools or collaborating with bilingual colleagues for support.

Acknowledge that teachers do not need to be fluent in every language their students speak. However, trying to learn and understand basic phrases and greetings can go a long way in building rapport with students and their families. This effort shows a willingness to embrace diversity and creates a welcoming environment for all.

Furthermore, recognize that language is not the only form of communication. Nonverbal cues, gestures, and visual aids can help facilitate understanding between students and teachers. Encouraging peer-to-peer interactions between students of different languages can also promote mutual understanding and learning.

Promoting multilingualism in the classroom is not about forcing students to speak a certain language but about creating an inclusive and supportive environment where all languages are valued. As educators, we can embrace diversity and empower our students through language.

THE HACK IN ACTION

*The following is an example from
Maurice McDavid's classroom.*

Teachers often use various forms of inspiration from pop culture to create engaging lessons. A great example is using rap music to teach the flexibility of words. Rap, a form of vocal delivery typically accompanied by a beat, utilizes wordplay and creative language to convey messages. In this example, Mr. McDavid incorporated rap into his lesson on wordplay to increase comprehension.

Mr. McDavid began by playing the song "Diamonds from Sierra Leone (remix)" by Kanye West. The students were asked to listen carefully to the lyrics and identify any phrases requiring an explanation. One chosen phrase included the words "businessman" and "business, man." Mr. McDavid explained that in this context, the word "businessman" refers to someone who works in business, while "business, man" means that someone sees themself as an entity or brand. This example highlights how words can have multiple meanings depending on the context. Grammar and language structure are lessons we can pull from this example.

Next, Mr. McDavid asked the students to come up with their own lyrics using vocabulary words from their unit. This activity allowed for creativity and encouraged students to expand their vocabulary in a fun and engaging way. Through this exercise, students could see how to manipulate and play with words to convey different meanings. Note that this was an economics lesson, and while the teacher did not necessarily view himself as a language arts teacher, he understood elements of language and how it can leverage student identity for learning.

It also highlights the importance of incorporating diverse cultural references into education and utilizing creative teaching methods to engage students. By embracing different forms of expression and exploring language in unconventional ways, educators can foster a more dynamic and inclusive learning environment for their students. Dynamic teachers continue to find innovative ways to connect with students and promote meaningful learning experiences. Teachers can create powerful lessons that resonate with students and enhance their understanding of language and communication by tapping into popular culture such as hip-hop, memes, social media, and video games.

For our Hack summaries, we ask you to ACT. That is, we offer you a few **Actions (A)** to take upon finishing the chapter, a few ideas for you to **Consider (C)**, and one reason to make this Hack a **Turning Point (T)** in your teaching.

Actions:

- Write down what you already know about language. Include where you learned these ideas, if applicable, and whether they have changed over time.

- Study a dialect of a language you speak. If it is English, you could research AAVE, Chicano English, British English, Cajun English, or another dialect.

- During your next week in a school setting, listen for what languages are used and how language is talked about. Listen for assumptions, whether positive or negative, made about people based on the way they speak.

Consider:

- Consider what impact language has on your identity and day-to-day interactions in the community where you live or serve. How might that experience be different for others?

- Consider how much, if at all, you talk about language in your classroom. Are there ways that you can increase the level of conversation about language without missing other content?

Turning Point:

- According to a 2020 article entitled "Teaching Culturally and Linguistically Diverse Students" posted on the School of Education website of American University, between 2010 and 2020, the percentage of non-White students in public schools grew from 48 percent to 54 percent. In the last twenty years, the number of students identified as English learners grew from around 8 percent to over 10 percent. This demographic shift represents why educators must begin to center language in their instruction across all grade levels and content areas. If we do not respond, we will continue to see the gaps in academic testing data and, ultimately, college and career readiness.

HACK
2

ALL EDUCATORS MUST BE LANGUAGE TEACHERS

Use English Learning Models for Students Who Speak Multiple Dialects

*To learn a new language is one more window
from which to look at the world.*
— CHINESE PROVERB

THE PROBLEM: STUDENTS COME TO SCHOOL NOT SPEAKING "SCHOOL ENGLISH"

ONE MIGHT ASSUME that students who speak English as their first, or even second, language come to school ready to learn from English-speaking teachers. A second part of this assumption is that if educators speak the same language as the students in front of them, the educators are ready to teach those students. Both assumptions are false. For years, students who identify as English language learners have trailed behind native English speakers on standardized English tests in particular, but all standardized tests as a whole. An additional example is that Black students' scores across the nation lag the national average on these same exams. These are statistical facts readily available on the National Education Center for Statistics website.

While it may be easier to rationalize the performance of students who may be learning the English language in the same year they are taking the assessment, many Black and Brown students have spent their entire lives speaking English. It is estimated acquiring a whole new language can take up to six years. What, however, is creating the problem with our students of color who grew up speaking "English"? While many factors undoubtedly play a role in this varied outcome on assessments, one overlooked consideration is the existing linguistic mismatch. Black students speak English. However, in many places across the United States and around the world, Black people speak a particular vernacular of English. Vernacular, as used here, is the native language as opposed to a second language. We will also use dialect interchangeably with this term. As mentioned in Chapter 1, Chicano English is another example of an English vernacular.

These differing versions of language are important because they appear in the classroom, particularly in reading instruction and assessment. In their 2021 article, "Teaching Black Children to Read," Julie A. Washington and Mark S. Seidenberg state that teaching reading is really the act of expressing the spoken word in a written fashion. There is an opportunity for a mismatch between the spoken language of students of color and the language of reading instruction.

When the language or vernacular spoken by students differs from the language being taught, it creates additional challenges not faced by students who speak and learn to read the same version of English. Students who need to learn "Standard English" should be considered bi-dialectical. Essentially, they speak two dialects of English.

THE HACK: ALL EDUCATORS MUST BE LANGUAGE TEACHERS

To some, the research-based strategies taught in English language learning certificate programs may seem like just "good teaching" and are helpful practices for *all* students. We agree—because we are *all* English language learners. None of us have mastered all the vocabulary to be mastered, nor do we all use standard grammar conventions correctly. Beyond that first simple truth, note that students come to school with varied exposures to Standard English. Still, students come to school with some kind of language. The following idea is simple and perhaps goes without saying, but sometimes, it is necessary to say it: All educators must be language teachers.

No one doubts that teaching language skills is a key component of a successful education system and, in turn, a prosperous nation. Going back to the founding of the United States, Thomas Jefferson argued that an educated populace is necessary for a democracy to function. While we understand his interpretation did not include all people groups, in our modern experience, we see the value of ensuring every student who comes through our school doors receives a high level of education.

Literacy is still at the core of education. Even with the vast array of formats in which one can find information, it's necessary to gain the ability to access, process, and apply learning from the written word. Unfortunately, we know the task of teaching reading is not evenly distributed among all teachers. We also know that the results of reading instruction are not equal among all students. This unintentional inequity does at least two things: it creates an opportunity gap between those students who can read and those who cannot, and it ultimately creates outcome gaps divided along that same line. Unfortunately, these gaps are not blind to color, ethnicity, home language, or family income. Surmounting such challenges can feel overwhelming.

A positive aspect is that this simple Hack—the intentional use of language learning strategies for students who speak languages or dialects other than SAE—can be a significant part of closing and eliminating those gaps.

USE TEXTS CONNECTED TO THE LOCAL COMMUNITY OR THE COMMUNITIES OF THE STUDENTS YOU SERVE.

Similar to working with students who come to school speaking a language other than English, this process begins with recognizing that the languages students use have rules and structure. This means we can build upon aspects of their languages to form a foundation for reading instruction. Therefore, teachers must have a basic understanding and awareness of the languages and dialects spoken in their classrooms. You might conduct a language survey or give students the opportunity to share information in their own voices, whether written or spoken. Hearing students speak in their voices can help teachers understand more about the students' levels of variance from Standard American English.

Ultimately, teachers' understanding will come through a study of the standards they need to teach and a comparative analysis of those standards and the languages that students bring into the classroom. You can find example organizers on our website, blackbrownbilingue.com, to help with that analysis. They are similar to a reading error analysis chart, which is commonly used to take notes as a student reads and list the types of errors they make, but instead focuses on linguistic or dialectical differences.

WHAT *YOU* CAN DO TOMORROW

Recognizing varying levels of experience with ELL instructional strategies, we are confident in your ability to make amazing linguistic things happen *tomorrow* for your students. The following surefire strategies will help you engage with your bilingual and bi-dialectical students in ways that will improve their reading and overall learning. They are ELL strategies adapted especially for students who already speak some form of English. However, you can use them with all students in your classroom.

- **Survey the class to discover the diverse linguistic backgrounds of your students.** Ask students, if they are old enough (or ask parents of younger students), what language is spoken in their home, even as a secondary language. While states require families to do a home language survey upon registering for school, languages are sometimes left off. Consider including survey questions that ask directly about the use of dialects other than SAE. To do this, try to remove any concepts of shame that are sometimes connected to language. Here is a sample survey introduction and questions that might be useful to build your understanding of dialects, vernacular, and other forms of non-standard English in your classroom.

Dear Parents and Families,

In our classroom this year, we will speak directly about the use of languages other than English and dialects other than the standard form of languages. Please answer the following questions about your students at home.

- *Do you and/or your children speak a language other than English at home? If so, what language?*

- *Do you and/or your children speak a dialect of English other than Standard American English? Some examples are Chicano English, African American Vernacular English, or Cajun Vernacular English.*

- *Do you or anyone in your family actively teach code-switching or intentionally speak differently based on where you are or in what context you are speaking?*

Thank you.

- **Focus on vocabulary in context.** Explicitly teach academic and content-specific vocabulary (if it's not already a part of your regular practice). Then ask students to process and apply this vocabulary, meaning the vocabulary practice must be more than rote memorization or flash card practice. Consider having the students explain the vocabulary in their own words to one another, emphasizing the meaning. Often, in the early grades, this includes adding grade-level-appropriate sight words. Again, to avoid having students be "word callers" or students who can decode a word but not make meaning from the word, these vocabulary words must be practiced in connection with their meanings.

- **Use culturally relevant texts.** Use texts connected to the local community or the communities of the students you serve. The local library is a great source for books written by local authors or about the local community. Additionally, plenty of sites provide lists of culturally responsive texts by topic. When students see themselves represented in the text they are using, they have higher student engagement and thus a greater amount of learning. In math, this may mean using agriculture as the basis for a math problem if your students come from backgrounds heavily involved in agriculture. Use a story the student connects to while teaching certain grammatical concepts, and the student will have a deeper attachment to the day's learning.

- **Directly compare students' spoken language with standard writing.** Because the teaching of reading is the teaching of a written code for a spoken language, this comparison allows students to note differences and be intentional about making the changes necessary to produce language in Standard American English. Teachers and students might work together to note the presence or absence of certain sounds in words as they are

> spoken and written. Consider this especially in science where students can benefit from learning prefixes and suffixes to help them understand and read technical words in that field. As you compare the language, be sure not to place added value on one or the other. Instead, emphasize that both types of language have value in different contexts.

A BLUEPRINT FOR FULL IMPLEMENTATION

Linguistic diversity in the classroom is rich with educational opportunities, and tapping into it begins with understanding the spectrum of languages students speak. Schools can employ various methods to uncover this linguistic landscape. Start with a detailed enrollment form that asks about the primary language spoken at home. Hold cultural heritage events where students can share about their linguistic backgrounds, and encourage dialogue between parents and teachers during meetings or through surveys. The following steps will help you do just that.

STEP 1: Acknowledge and learn about the linguistic diversity in your school and classroom.

This step is paramount to having a deeper understanding of your students as language learners. Although educators typically reserve the term "language learners" for students from homes where a language other than English is spoken, note that all people are developing language. Surveys, conversations about home languages, and direct observations of your students' language use are great ways to discover their linguistic strengths. The following list includes students' potential linguistic strengths and areas that need further development.

- knowledge of multiple languages/dialects
- ability to code-switch between languages
- strong listening and speaking skills
- ability to recognize and produce different sounds
- understanding of different grammatical structures or syntax
- ability to communicate effectively in different contexts

STEP 2: Connect with others to build your English language learner toolkit.

Once you secure information about students' languages when entering your classroom, you will need to gather strategies to support your students. The tools necessary to support an English language learner are almost always present in a school building. Your colleagues are great resources for in-house, on-the-job professional development. Tap into the resources of fellow educators to help support your students with diverse linguistic backgrounds.

STEP 3: Start small but be intentional about including these practices.

Often, educators feel trapped by the overwhelming number of strategies recommended to support their students, so it's key to start small. Choose one or two tools that you believe will be effective with your students, and practice those. Implementing these strategies will do two things: it will give you the chance to get better at implementing the tool and it will give you time to see if the practice is working. If it's not the right tool for your students or your classroom, change it. As you develop units and plan lessons, include these tools as an intentional part of your planning.

A great example is the intentional use of vocabulary in context, as we mentioned in the previous section. Throw out the vocabulary flash cards and give vocabulary lessons as part of other lessons. Try these strategies:

- Add a word box at the bottom of an assignment to capture new vocabulary.

- Use sentence stems to help students form grammatically standard sentences.

- Include the rules of a student's dialect as a specific teaching point for direct instruction in language. For example, in the previously mentioned article, "Teaching Black Children to Read," Julie A. Washington mentions that in African American English, the "g" is often dropped from the ending of gerunds. This detail provides a perfect opportunity for a teaching point about gerunds and their spelling in SAE.

STEP 4: Expand these practices by integrating them into the curriculum.

With enough practice, you will feel comfortable using more than just one or two of these practices, and you may use these practices more deeply. Try these strategies:

- Conduct a metalinguistic comparative analysis of SAE and the other dialects/languages spoken in the classroom.
  - ▶ Think and talk about language in your classroom, comparing how the rules are similar, how they are different, and how they function in communicating effectively.

> ▶ A comparative analysis is an excellent tool for language learning, but it requires a deeper understanding of language acquisition. You'll find a video on our website that explains metalinguistic comparative analysis and modeling. As you repeat these strategies and gain expertise, you can build them into your lesson plan without hesitation.

- Use total physical response (TPR).

  > ▶ Imagine teaching a social studies lesson that is heavy in content-specific vocabulary. In the past, you may have given students a list of words with their matching definitions, but now you can adapt the lesson with language learning strategies.

  > ▶ TPR is a great strategy to integrate into social studies or science. It's about connecting the words and definitions with a matching physical action. In this way, the students have a movement that connects to the content they are learning.

- Use figurative language to define a vocabulary word or a new concept.

  > ▶ For vocabulary practice, an additional strategy is the action of creating a metaphor that describes the word. For example, the leaves are the food factory of the tree. These repeated strategies give students a sense of normalcy in their learning and offer variety in how students interact with the learning.

STEP 5: Continue to reflect on, collaborate, and assess the impact of these practices.

Too often, we endeavor to make too many strategic changes. Additionally, we may not allow ourselves the time to reflect on the impact of these changes. Minimize the number of strategies and measure their impact through student assessment data and qualitative conversations with colleagues. Here are a few questions for teachers to consider:

- Based on the student data, what are the students' linguistic needs?

- What specific strategies support meeting students' needs?

- How will success be determined? (Here, consider student assessment data and the ways in which students can share how they feel about their learning.)

- What will happen if students succeed? What will happen if they do not?

For schools that already have a professional learning community (PLC) model, it is an ideal place for this reflection to happen. You may also consider conversations with school leaders or members of a School Improvement Team (SIT). Student assessment data and survey data, where students share how they feel about their language learning, would be great information to review; consider implementing a short reflection survey at the end of each unit of instruction, for example. Move learning forward, especially for your students with more complex needs.

INTEGRATING LANGUAGE INSTRUCTION DOES NOT ADD TO YOUR PLATE; IT CHANGES WHAT IS ON YOUR PLATE.

OVERCOMING PUSHBACK

Educators often contend with a perpetual addition of responsibilities, requiring a multifaceted approach and a compassionate view of the pressures and time constraints of the job. Teachers tasked with integrating language instruction, for instance, might feel that it intensifies existing expectations or perpetuates lower standards for marginalized groups. Those feelings are valid; without question, we should acknowledge this challenge. However, when educators see the tangible benefits of their efforts, such as improved student outcomes and a more inclusive environment, they're more likely to feel empowered rather than burdened by the additional tasks. To see positive results, however, we must be willing to start and continue this practice. Here are a few common concerns about this Hack and how to address them.

Integrating language instruction is just another task for teachers. We all can agree that a major goal of schools across our nation is to create more proficient readers. The model of incorporating language is one way to address Tier One instruction, potentially decreasing the number of students of color or impoverished students identified for special education. It's another way to do things, not an additional way to do things. Integrating language instruction does not add to your plate; it changes what is on your plate. Stop doing what is not working and begin doing something different.

Linguistic teaching allows for lower standards for our poor students and students of color. It's quite the opposite. We can't stress enough that the purpose of the strategies outlined here is to encourage students and teachers to honor and value home languages while recognizing that they don't always match the learning expectations of the school. We aim to promote clear feedback to students about their learning. It also allows students to actively compare their spoken languages or home languages with the language of instruction, and it roots student learning in long-term memory. Once more, this must be done without devaluing one language or another. Instead, celebrate the idea that students are bi-dialectical or bilingual.

I don't know anything about language acquisition or my students' languages. There is no simple solution to this, and it undoubtedly will require work on the teacher's part. However, many teachers ask questions of their students and families at the beginning of the year. Apart from the already mandatory Home Language Survey currently required by federal law, this Hack gives teachers different questions to ask of their families. Remember that sample classroom-level home language questions are listed in the prior What You Can Do Tomorrow section. In that same way, teachers already collaborate with their colleagues and participate in job-embedded professional development. This Hack gives teachers a different focus for why and with whom they might collaborate. As teachers continue to learn more about their school's diverse linguistic landscape, they become better equipped to meet the needs of their diverse students.

THE HACK IN ACTION

*The following is a true story, and the
teacher's name is a pseudonym.*

Ms. Libson was a veteran kindergarten teacher. She had seen and overcome many challenges excellently over her nearly twenty-year career. The district where she served had always had an incredibly high number of students identified as English language learners (ELL). However, since an overwhelming majority of these students were Spanish speaking, they were served through the dual language program. Ms. Libson taught a monolingual instruction classroom. And though she had a handful of ELL students, all the students in her classroom had English as their dominant language. She knew how to teach kindergarten students to read, both for bilingual students and those who spoke only English.

One January, the situation changed when she received two new students who were African American. In a school where the student population was less than 3 percent Black, it was notable. They were twin girls who brought a myriad of social-emotional learning (SEL) concerns. They struggled to regulate their emotions when other students bothered them and academic tasks challenged them. An additional concern was that these students had not yet learned to read. As Ms. Libson did initial assessments, she found that the twin girls had not yet acquired many foundational skills. What's more, even after four weeks of instruction, the students still struggled to learn new material. Ms. Libson brought her concerns about the girls to her PLC group, which included her principal and the building instructional coach.

In that meeting, her instructional coach recommended some strategies included in this Hack. Ms. Libson had not yet spent much time talking with the mom because she knew the mom was busy trying to get acclimated to the new district and city. The parent conversation was the first step. The mom shared that she was a struggling reader herself. Ms. Libson noted that the mom used different components of AAVE in her communication. With this in mind, the teacher, coach, and principal hatched a plan to implement specific strategies for language learners.

In this situation, Ms. Libson began with the explicit instruction of vocabulary and increased exposure to rich language input. She worked with the students on describing new vocabulary in their home language. She also utilized extra adults in the classroom to read with these students, giving them a chance to hear more SAE in the context of literacy. With these two strategies, with the ongoing instruction of phonics, the students quickly advanced in their reading. Through these linguistic strategies, the sisters did not have to enter the multi-tiered system of supports (MTSS) Tier 2 intervention, academic supports for students who are not achieving with the instruction happening for the whole class.

Once again, we will ask you to ACT. We fully recognize that this Hack asks you to engage in even more personal learning and professional development. While we have made recommendations in this chapter and have provided resources on our website, blackbrownbilingue.com, we wholeheartedly believe that those who will get the most out of this Hack will complete the following Actions, Consider the following ideas, and make a decision that this is, indeed, a Turning Point for how they will interact with linguistically diverse students.

Actions:

- Learn about the linguistic diversity of your district. The best resources are those who teach language learners or run the language learning program.

- Choose a dialect of American English and learn about it. A Google search will suffice to get you started along your learning journey.

- Research the socio-political and historical impact of language on the education system.

Consider:

- Consider how you have previously served linguistically diverse students not identified as ESL/ELL. Have you considered the home language of students who speak a variation of English while in school?

- Consider the changes you need to make to your current instruction planning and implementation in order to utilize this Hack successfully.

- Consider the ways you can be a part of making our educational system more linguistically responsive.

Turning Point:

- The reason this can be a turning point in your career is part learning science and part social science. As for the first part (learning science), according to a 2023 article by Dana Leon for HMH, "Effective Strategies: Scaffolding for ELL Students That Benefits the Whole Class," ELL strategies benefit all students in the classroom, including those who are learning the language of instruction, even if not as a second language. As for the second part (social science) of the reason this can be a turning point in your career, teachers often spend hours planning lessons for the whole class and then make adaptations for students in various student groups. However, this Hack proposes that you could start your planning with ELLs in mind and use those strategies for all students, differentiated as necessary. This method would save time and energy in the planning process, increasing efficiency.

HACK
3

TALK TOGETHER, LEARN TOGETHER

Incorporate Collectivist Talk Structures in School

The nature of man is a dual nature. He must be both an individualist and a collectivist.
— OFTEN ATTRIBUTED TO WINSTON CHURCHILL, BRITISH STATESMAN

THE PROBLEM: THE EMPHASIS IS ON THE INDIVIDUAL IN SCHOOLS

ACCORDING TO THE National Center for Educational Statistics, over 50 percent of the students in American schools are students of color. Black students comprise 15 percent of the population, while Hispanic children comprise 28 percent. These two numbers do not include Asian, multiracial, and

Indigenous students. As our student population continues to diversify, we will see more students come from collectivist backgrounds.

Collectivist cultures are those that have a strong group orientation, value collaboration over competition, and see relationships as fundamental to learning and business. See Table 1. The top five collectivist countries in the world are in Latin America, including Colombia, Venezuela, Panama, Ecuador, and Guatemala, with the latter rated the most collectivist. On the other hand, the United States tops the list of the most individualistic nations, followed by New Zealand, the Netherlands, Australia, and the United Kingdom.

COLLECTIVIST VS. INDIVIDUALIST CULTURES

Concepts	Collectivism	Individualism
Self-Perception	Describes self in terms of roles and relationships. "I am because we are."	Describes self in terms of characteristics, "I think therefore I am."
Community	Relationships are valued above all else.	Relationships can be seen as a means to an end.
Achievement	The achievement of the community is more important than the individual. Collaboration is key.	The achievement of the individual is key to success. Meritocracy is valued. Competition is key.
Priorities	The family, the community, in some cases conformity.	The immediate family, individual achievement, and standing out.
Countries	Colombia, Venezuela, Panama, China, Ghana.	United States, United Kingdom, Australia, Netherlands.

Table 1

Another way these cultural differences impact people is through relationships. In a collectivist culture, building relationships with new people is more challenging because it is more difficult to meet them. Strangers are more likely to remain strangers in a collective culture because most relationships are formed due to factors such as family and geographical location instead of personal choice. This aspect of the culture is not inherently good or bad, but worth noting as you consider the students coming into your classroom.

While the overall traits and characteristics of a collectivist culture seem more altruistic, there are potential pitfalls. For example, collectivistic cultures may foster socially reticent or withdrawn behaviors. Again, remembering that individuals in collectivist cultures do not tend to want to stand out can explain why individuals from these cultures can become socially withdrawn. This factor leads to less social support because people in collectivist cultures tend to be more cautious about sharing personal problems with friends or trusted adults. Instead, people from collectivist cultures tend to spend more time with supportive family and friends.

> COLLECTIVIST TALK STRUCTURES FOCUS ON COLLABORATION, COMMUNITY, AND COMMUNICATION, ENABLING STUDENTS TO WORK TOGETHER TO ARRIVE AT A COMMON UNDERSTANDING.

So, how does this apply to schools? Cultural nuances impact oral and written traditions, meaning they will manifest in the classroom. Some cultures have relied on spoken language instead of written language to convey, preserve, and share knowledge from one generation to the next. Oral traditions place a heavy emphasis on relationships because the process connects the speaker and the listener in a community, whereas written traditions do not require much person-to-person interaction.

Schools are like a petri dish where all these cultural nuances either thrive or die. Those in an environment conducive to growth, whether in a petri dish or a school, will survive. Those not in an environment conducive to growth will not thrive because the environment is incompatible with their needs. This scenario happens to certain student populations repeatedly. As a result, schools and districts spend thousands of dollars on school improvement efforts, such as hiring consultants, buying new materials, and providing training and professional development. Unfortunately, those efforts often do not target the issue and show little promise toward improving student performance.

People could give more consideration to the role of collectivist talk structures in any given organization, especially in comparison to individualistic structures. When students from collectivist backgrounds come into schools that center individualism, conflicts can arise, leading to arguments and fights because the students may not understand or appreciate each other's communication styles. For instance, a student from a collectivist culture may interpret an individualist student's directness as rude or aggressive.

In contrast, an individualist student might view the indirectness of a collectivist student as passive-aggressive behavior. Students may withdraw from class interactions, as they do not feel supported by their classmates. Teachers may feel like students are being disrespectful as the teachers endeavor to support or seek support from other students. These issues show up in classrooms all the time.

THE HACK: TALK TOGETHER, LEARN TOGETHER

Implementing collectivist talk structures in the classroom can improve student learning and engagement. Collectivist talk structures focus on collaboration, community, and communication, enabling students to work together to arrive at a common understanding. This type of talk structure is markedly different from the more individualistic approach often found in classrooms, where students are expected to generate their ideas independently. Note that individual talk structures are also valuable. They are, however, connected to the dominant culture of schools and thus are much more likely to be already present. This Hack aims to balance individualist and collectivist talk structures by finding an equilibrium between the two.

Collectivist talk structures allow everyone's voice to be heard and valued equally. When every voice is appreciated, students feel more connected to one another and to the material they are learning. It creates an environment of understanding and respect that encourages meaningful discussion, problem-solving, and critical thinking. Furthermore, it allows for multiple perspectives to be shared, creating a well-rounded educational experience for all involved. In many ways, this may sound like the concept of restorative practices that include restorative circles. That makes sense, considering that restorative circles are said to have their roots in Indigenous cultures, which tend to be collectivist. However, many people think of restorative practices as related to school discipline, while collectivist talk structures also can and should be used to increase oracy during academic instruction.

In practice, teachers can use various techniques to promote collectivist talk structures in the classroom. Structured conversations such as Socratic seminars or think-pair-share can encourage student collaboration while stimulating critical thinking skills. Additionally, when teaching content, teachers can strive to ask open-ended questions rather than ones with definitive answers; this further encourages discussion between students and supports collective problem-solving skills.

While schools and classrooms may already use these strategies, it is paramount to understand that the strategies' impact may differ depending on students' cultures. Students coming from collectivist cultures likely process information better through discussion and conversation. As noted earlier, many Latin American countries have collectivist cultures. Language and culture are often inseparable, so collectivist talk structures give students learning

SAE a culturally responsive method to practice both the language aspect of their learning and the mastery of content.

Collectivist talk structures empower all learners, regardless of their backgrounds or individual capabilities, by providing a platform for shared knowledge and understanding across different environments. In addition, they improve students' confidence levels by creating an interconnected learning space that focuses on working together rather than competing against each other. These strategies allow everyone's voice to be heard and enable students to build relationships, a skill necessary long after they leave the classroom.

WHAT *YOU* CAN DO TOMORROW

We understand that not everyone feels well-versed in addressing the collectivist cultures of students. It can also feel overwhelming to consider both individualistic and collectivist nuances on your own. Do not fret! The following ideas will help you incorporate collectivist talk structures in your practice. Some may already be common practices in your classroom, but retooling them with language needs and your students' diverse linguistic cultures in mind will only enhance the quality of conversations and learning.

- **Use more Socratic seminars.** Socratic seminars are an excellent tool for igniting critical thinking skills and dialogue. With the implementation of the Common Core State Standards came an emphasis on speaking and listening skills that was not present prior to the rollout. These seminars are a great way to tap into students' prior knowledge and connect it with new information. It also requires students to substantiate any claims they make by providing evidence. Socratic seminars foster the ability to think from multiple perspectives, a skill that has become increasingly necessary to navigate our world.

So, how do you implement a Socratic seminar? You can structure it in various ways, and here is a basic structure that you can adapt. All students must read the same text prior to the seminar. Then the class sits in two circles: one inner and one outer circle. The students inside the circle respond to a question posed by the group leader. Notably, the group leader is *never* the teacher; instead, it's another student. As the inner circle discusses the question, the outside circle observes and takes notes. Students in the outer circle are to note:

▸ What the participants were doing as others were speaking.

▸ How many times each person in the inner circle spoke.

▸ The ideas shared during the seminar. Were there several different ideas, or was the dialogue focused on one or two ideas?

▸ Any participant who changed their opinion as a result of the evidence presented in the seminar.

▸ How many times a participant responded to or added on to the remarks of another participant.

Once completed, the process is repeated with the outside circle rotating to the inside. Once everyone has had an opportunity to participate in both inside and outside circles, they reflect on the seminar. Post-seminar reflective questions might include:

▸ What did you do well during the seminar?

▸ What could you work on to be a stronger participant?

▸ How did your thinking grow or change because of your participation in the seminar?

▸ Did you go into the seminar with any unanswered questions or confusion? How was your thinking clarified?

▸ Describe the actions taken by the person you feel was the strongest participant in the discussion. How did they keep the conversation moving while engaging others' thinking?

• **Play games that include oracy.** We cannot overstate the benefit of games. Not only do they engage learners in a fun way, but they also help develop oral language skills. Students, especially those from diverse language backgrounds, tend to have a high affective filter when speaking. According to *Colorín Colorado*, a site for educators of English language learners, the affective filter describes a learner's attitudes that affect the relative success of second language acquisition. If a student has negative feelings about learning, such as a lack of motivation, a lack of self-confidence, and learning anxiety, it can hinder and obstruct language learning.

Games have been shown to lower this affective filter and promote the spontaneous use of language. They also help increase communicative competence. Games are student-centered and can lead to whole-class cohesion, which is precisely the type of environment students from collectivist cultures need to thrive in the classroom. Games can be easily adapted and adjusted based on content, age, and the ability of a group.

- **Value storytelling.** Students from collectivist cultures tend to be accustomed to teaching and learning through storytelling. Storytelling is an ancient practice of passing down knowledge, culture, and history. By allowing students to teach and learn through storytelling, teachers can make note of observable patterns, unspoken rules, and underlying beliefs and values. Our brains are wired for stories. The brain's neurons light up when we are told a story, in the language processing parts and in other regions, as if we were performing the action ourselves. For example, if someone in a story is running or jumping, the motor regions of our brain light up. When we intertwine stories with new information, learning is much more likely to take place.

- **Emphasize peer support.** Students from collectivist backgrounds view helping others as their obligation. For example, a teacher in a dual language classroom may assign jobs to two students per class after noticing that her students often volunteer support to their peers without being asked first. It's one example of a student-initiated approach to classroom jobs. Another way teachers can emphasize peer support is by creating a rule that no one is finished with a task until everyone is finished. Finally, if the class average increases, students can receive a bump in their grade. Because students from a collectivist culture tend to value community success over individual success, this practice may help to engage these students in the learning more deeply. These are simple ways to institutionalize collectivism.

- **Create routines of affirmation.** Develop weekly meetings for students to affirm each other's identity or express gratitude to one another. Make sure to develop processes so all students are included and none are left out. Some iterations that currently exist in classrooms are "student of the week" or "star student," in which students are praised and affirmed by their classmates. You can choose this approach or the more organic approach of having all students affirm their peers weekly. These weekly affirmations could occur during a daily class meeting or once a week as part of the class arrival routine. Students could take turns leading it each week. Whatever you choose, this is a practice that will change the dynamics of your classroom for the better.

- **Plan with the group in mind.** When teachers plan group activities, they often find that some students inevitably take over the task while others assume a more passive role. Other times, students work on a group project parallel to each other rather than reaping the benefits of group work. When planning a culminating project or task, plan with the group in mind, meaning you assign critical interdependence roles to students. Examples include peer feedback, collaborative decision-making and problem-solving, and consensus-building. Various tools can help you with this; at its core, it's about developing a collectivist mindset. One great tool is the book *Hacking Group Work* by Connie Hamilton from the *Hack Learning Series*.

A BLUEPRINT FOR FULL IMPLEMENTATION

In the classroom setting, teachers aiming to foster increased student achievement for all students, no matter their linguistic or cultural background, can integrate collectivist talk structures by promoting dialogue that emphasizes collaboration, shared goals, and mutual support. While this may feel daunting, we hope the following concepts will help you along the way.

STEP 1: Take an inventory of which collectivist talk structures you already have in your repertoire.

First, understand that collectivist talk structures are forms of communication that prioritize collaboration and interdependence among group members. This type of communication helps foster an environment where all group members contribute to the discussion and feel respected while they do so.

To take an inventory, observe how you interact with others when in group settings. Do you often lead the conversation or open up space for others to join in? Do you ask questions to gain clarification on others' thoughts or opinions? Can you listen actively, process what has been said, and contribute further understanding or insight?

Additionally, consider how well you work with others to accomplish a task or reach a goal. Can you divide tasks among the group so everyone works toward the same result? Last, reflect on how well you manage conflicts within a group setting. Can you step back from your thoughts and feelings and try to see from another person's perspective? Communication can be tricky, but by assessing these skills, you can build more effective collective talk structures with your peers and students and help your students identify their own inventories.

STEP 2: Seek learning opportunities for desired practices.

Researching collectivist practices in professional development can be an eye-opening experience. Key search phrases include:

- increasing oracy
- classroom talk structures
- Kagan Cooperative Learning Structures
- collaborative classroom structures

The idea of getting students to interact with one another in class is certainly not new, but when you better understand the "why" behind its impact on your students, it helps you plan and implement it better.

Consider making this learning a target of your professional learning community or your collaborative plan time with your team. Work with your colleagues who have already had success implementing these strategies. As mentioned in Chapter 2, working with your ESL-certified teachers and administrators will help you find more practices to implement. In ESL classrooms across the United States, increasing student oracy is a goal, as it helps to produce quicker language uptake. With that in mind, those colleagues are excellent sources of ways to expand communicative and collaborative classroom practices.

STEP 3: Seek feedback from your students and invite them to join the process.

Students' initial response to the increased utilization of collectivist talk structures may not be cheering because these structures require students to think about and then formulate their own ideas. This practice can be challenging for students who may be used to instruction that falls under the pattern of "sit and get" and regurgitate. Every classroom teacher, if honest, can think of a lesson in which they talked at the students for far too long. During these speeches, it is likely that some linguistically diverse students missed parts of the content. This situation is where these structures come in. Allowing students the time to process this new learning by talking through it with peers is an excellent way to connect the novel information with what they already know. However, if you are not getting feedback from the students, you will not know if the structures are having their full effect.

Invite students to reflect on the structures selected for information processing in the day's lesson. To start, ask your students the following questions:

- Were you able to describe the new learning in a way that made sense to you? Did it make sense to your peers?

- What did you like about the structure of the conversation? What was challenging?

- What could I do, as the facilitator, to help you engage better in this structure?

- Is there another way that you feel you could express your learning better?

That last question leaves space for students from a more individualistic background to still feel heard, and it gives the teacher permission to adjust either unit to unit or student to student.

Finally, hear ideas from your students in terms of how to structure these conversations or collaborative practices. Students at the secondary level who travel from class to class may have ideas to share about engaging experiences in other classes. For administrators, collecting these ideas from students and then trying them out in a staff meeting is a valuable way to expose staff to new, student-driven ideas.

WORKING TOGETHER CAN HELP BREAK DOWN LEARNING BARRIERS BY ALLOWING FOR MORE DIVERSE PERSPECTIVES AND APPROACHES TOWARD STUDYING.

OVERCOMING PUSHBACK

Much of the pushback for this Hack is rooted in a desire to maintain the status quo in classrooms. Teachers have inevitable and valid concerns about taking time away from addressing content. They may worry about a student's ability to perform on a content-specific task. They may feel uneasy about the idea of effectively assessing students working in student-centered talk structures. Fortunately, the following ideas will help you get beyond these potential roadblocks.

Students need to build independent skills because this is what the real world expects of them. We often rationalize our actions by stating that we are preparing students for the real world. Yes, students need to be held accountable, develop their independence, and be responsible. But if we look at what the "real world" expects of them, you will see that to be able to collaborate is of the utmost importance.

When students can work with their peers, they gain a better understanding of the content, process new information more effectively, and develop increased problem-solving skills. Some may say that with the internet and remote work, we have less of a need for collaboration. What we have learned is that even while working remotely, collaboration is critical. Working together can help break down learning barriers by allowing for more diverse perspectives and approaches toward studying.

Collaboration also helps facilitate student engagement and provides an environment for meaningful peer interaction. By engaging in collaborative activities, students gain valuable academic skills and develop social-emotional skills such as communication, teamwork, conflict resolution, and leadership. Furthermore, collaboration among classmates fosters stronger relationships between them and creates a sense of community within the classroom.

As we continue to see the landscape of our workforce evolve, it is becoming more common for people to work with individuals on the other side of the globe or from different backgrounds. Awareness of the cultural nuances beneath the surface will allow people to work together more harmoniously. Moreover, as some of our students go on to manage, supervise, or lead others, they need to know the different backgrounds and linguistic identities within an organization in order to lead successfully.

It will be difficult for me to assess their learning if they discuss things together. Grading group assignments can be tricky for teachers. To ensure fairness, teachers need to create a system that allows them to evaluate each student's individual contribution and assess their understanding of the material equitably. One effective method is to assign each student in the group a specific job or to contribute an equal amount of work toward the assignment. For example, one student could be appointed as the project manager while another might take on the role of proofreader. This way, all students are held accountable since the teacher will assess their individual contributions when grading time rolls around.

Teachers can also have students create rubrics to serve as a guideline for how their work should be evaluated, allowing them to provide clear expectations while monitoring progress. The teacher could also provide periodic anonymous surveys or check-ins to get an accurate picture of how much each team member has contributed to completing the assignment. This practice fosters transparency and eliminates potential biases in grading decisions. You can find an example survey on our website, blackbrownbilingue.com, in the blog post "Collectivist Cultures in the Classroom: Why We Need More Group Work."

Finally, teachers must grade group assignments holistically, looking at how well the work was completed and assessing if the students learned from the experience and questioned their assumptions about group dynamics. For students who are still striving toward a higher level of performance in their command of SAE, they can reflect on how their ideas were captured and transformed by their peers further along in that area. By grading assignments with this higher level of scrutiny, teachers can encourage teamwork, collaboration, and creative problem-solving skills among their students that will benefit them long after graduation.

THE HACK IN ACTION

The following anecdote is about a former teacher of author Lissette Jacobson. We have used a pseudonym for this teacher.

Mrs. Williams was a high school English teacher with over twenty years of experience in education. Throughout her career, she had seen firsthand the importance of creating an inclusive and collaborative classroom environment. However, it wasn't until she attended a professional development workshop on collectivist talk structures that she realized how powerful these structures could be in promoting student engagement and learning.

With her newfound knowledge, Mrs. Williams was determined to implement collectivist talk structures in her classroom. She started by introducing the concept to her students and explaining why it was important for them to work together and learn from one another. She also stressed that everyone's ideas and opinions were valuable and should be respected.

Mrs. Williams gradually introduced the new structures in her lessons to ensure a successful implementation. She started with small-group discussions, then moved on to whole-class discussions and debates. She also incorporated activities such as think-pair-share and jigsaw, where students had to work together to complete tasks and share their findings with the rest of the class.

Mrs. Williams provided clear instructions and guidelines for each activity, as well as designated roles for each student within the group, to create a sense of responsibility and accountability among the students. She ensured that everyone actively participated in the discussions.

The impact of using collectivist talk structures in Mrs. Williams's classroom was almost immediate. Students who were previously shy or quiet, including those in the "quiet phase" of language acquisition, started to actively participate in class discussions, sharing their thoughts and ideas with their peers. The quiet stage of acquiring a second language can occur when students have enough of the target language to communicate, but not without mistakes. Their anxiety around making mistakes can cause them to refrain from participating. Students also began to listen more attentively to one another and show respect for different perspectives. Mrs. Williams noticed that her students were becoming more confident in expressing themselves and taking ownership of their learning.

By implementing collectivist talk structures, Mrs. Williams created a more inclusive and collaborative classroom environment and saw improvements in her students' academic performance. Students could learn from one another's ideas and perspectives, leading to deeper understanding and critical thinking skills. Additionally, students developed essential communication and teamwork skills that would benefit them beyond the classroom.

In the face of an ever-diversifying school system in the United States, we must endeavor to recognize the deeper levels of culture that exist beyond food, celebrations, and clothing. Understanding the difference between collectivism and individualism is a valuable first step. Whereas in traditional classroom settings, teachers often lead discussions and students are expected to passively listen and take notes, we know this type of one-way communication is not always conducive to learning. We must be inclusive of more collaborative and student-centered teaching methods, including collectivist talk structures.

Actions:

- Learn about the collectivist cultures represented in your school and community, looking for patterns of communication that may already exist in your students' lives.

- Set a goal for the number of times per week you will include opportunities for students to engage in oral, collective information processing.

Consider:

- Consider how you create your groups when students do group work. Sometimes, it helps to have two students learning SAE work together to support one another. At other times, you may want to pair the SAE learner with a student with a high level of proficiency in SAE.

- Consider the rubrics you may already use to assess student note-taking. Could they be used to assess student discussions?

Turning Point:

- The reason this should be a turning point in your career is that we have all sat in meetings as adults where information was presented to us, and we were never given the chance to process it. Using these collectivist talk structures helps your linguistically diverse students and reinforces the idea that students can only take in new information for so long before their brains become overloaded. Stop and let the students process new information as it comes in.

HACK
4

ANALYZE YOUR ASSESSMENTS
Provide Multiple Modalities for Students to Show Mastery

What we see changes what we know. What we know changes what we see.
— JEAN PIAGET, PSYCHOLOGIST

THE PROBLEM: TESTS AND ESSAYS ARE NOT ONE-SIZE-FITS-ALL FOR STUDENTS

EVERY EDUCATOR HAS been surprised by the outcomes of an assessment, especially when the results did not match the students' performance during discussions or other activities in class where the students shined. And while both writing and test-taking skills are essential to success in our modern educational setting, those assessment methods do not always get at the crux of the learning. Generally, those methods can assess qualities other than the students' understanding of the focus standards, particularly for our culturally and linguistically diverse students. There are multiple reasons why this problem exists.

Hack 3 introduced the idea of collectivism, and its tenets play a significant role in understanding why essays are not the best way to assess some students. Again, collectivism, as juxtaposed to individualism, tends to center oral language more than written and the group more than the individual. It then becomes clear how an essay flies in the face of these deep cultural norms.

The essay asks students to work as individuals in the production of connected and synthesized ideas. Additionally, a student from a collectivist culture may be able to orally explain the information you are looking for but will struggle to produce something in writing. These are skills that the student can and should learn, but it must be noted that often, the student needs to learn both the content and the expectations around writing the essay. Even then, the bi-dialectical student (as discussed in Hack 2) needs to produce written language for school in SAE, "translating" it from the language they speak more naturally. All these ideas present as issues in the essay writing process.

The typical multiple-choice or true/false test is limited in the information it can collect and its ability to cement the learning. One major concern with tests is that they only ask students to recall information long enough to perform well on the tests, and then the students can forget it. This structure is different from what many of our culturally and linguistically diverse students need. They need a way to demonstrate their deep learning. While much of the Western world worships the written word, it is not the only way to show one's learning. With the flood of technological advancements, information is increasingly shared in many more ways. The bottom line is that as educators, we should have plenty of concerns about our easy essays and typical tests. We must consider other ways.

THE HACK: ANALYZE YOUR ASSESSMENTS

While assessing students through multiple modes is common, it is also not put into practice enough. Teachers can determine students' mastery of learning targets in various ways that far exceed the use of tests or traditional essays. The skills students need to finish a test or write an essay do not align well with most workforce tasks.

There are multiple reasons to assess your students in different ways. One consideration is that it allows for student choice. Student choice promotes student engagement and agency. Students feel they have a say in what happens in their classroom and how they will show their learning. This autonomy is especially important for our most vulnerable students who may not feel a strong sense of belonging in the school building or classroom.

Another reason to widen the array of assessments is that it allows students to lean into their strengths. Psychologist Howard Gardner introduced his theory of multiple intelligences in his 1983 book, *Frames of Mind: The Theory of Multiple Intelligences*. While his theoretical framework has been critiqued, it has also gained popularity among educators, who know without a doubt that students have certain modes of communication in which they feel stronger. Ultimately, that is what "assessment" is about. It is a method of communicating new learning to the teacher. A student who is a strong oral communicator may soar when given the opportunity to demonstrate learning through a presentation. That same student may partner with another who feels confident about presenting information in an organized and easy-to-understand way. Between the two students, one can lead in creating the presentation while the other can lead in presenting the information. Yet still, another student may have a strength in the arts, creative writing, or video production. All of these communication modes allow the students' strengths to be on full display.

Using assessments other than tests and essays is another way to center student interests. It is nearly impossible to consider student interests when using a traditional test. Even with an essay assessment, the parameters often restrict our students' abilities to showcase their learning because the essay requires them to write within the realm of a specific topic. Consider, however, how educators can emphasize students' interests when they assess students in more open-ended ways. Again, the downside of traditional tests and essays is that they ask for specific information. Other assessments allow the students to choose the information that connected to them the most and then demonstrate the skills and content knowledge using their own interests.

Think of a social studies class as an example. One of the fifth-grade history standards for the state of Illinois reads "SS.3–5.IS.1. Develop essential questions and expand the importance of the questions to self and others." The standardized test for this standard might present a multiple-choice question, such as:

> *Which of the following is an essential question about the Civil War?*
> *a. When did the Civil War start?*
> *b. How many people died fighting in the Civil War?*
> *c. What were the causes of the Civil War?*
> *d. When the US was fighting World War I, what lessons did it take from previous wars?*

We have several concerns about that question. The first is that the question does not allow for an expansion on the importance of the question. The second relates to student interests. If a student was asked to create an essential question about the Civil War with a group of friends and then create a podcast in which the classmates expanded their conversation about it, students could choose an area that interested them, connected to the Civil War. Some educators may call this project-based learning. Students given this option might choose, "What role did women play in the North and South during wartime?" or even, "What were the major military advancements made during the Civil War?" That student interest will result in higher student engagement and a higher chance that students will perform at a level necessary to meet or exceed the standard. We must endeavor to engage students intellectually in instruction and in assessment.

We can do this through more effective modes of assessment. Students need the opportunity to flex their brains; assessments that require the synthesis and application of new learning increase the likelihood that the learning will move from short-term to long-term memory. Whereas the typical tests ask for information to be regurgitated in isolation from the content being learned, other assessment modalities allow the students to connect the new learning to the schema that already exists and, in turn, to gather a new perspective. Although the discussion of this Hack in practice has already begun, please see the following specific examples of assessing students using different modalities and across subject areas.

- **Give a speech promoting a public policy.** In a typical career, a person is not asked to work with only one school subject at a time. So, this assessment allows teachers to intentionally integrate subject areas, asking students to think about how the main content they are learning is connected to other areas.

  ▶ *Science:* Students could prepare a speech using the science they have learned in a unit to argue for or against a particular public policy. This practice gives our language learners an opportunity to practice newly acquired academic vocabulary and do so orally. The ACCESS test, an English proficiency test, asks ELLs to perform in the speaking domain, specifically expecting them to use science and social studies vocabulary.

► *Math:* Students can meet the measurement and data standards by presenting a speech about expanding a local airport. Once students have created a scale map, they can determine how much additional area would be needed and the proximity of the planes to homes when taking off and landing.

► *Social studies:* Students could review public policies from various geographic locations or moments in history, compare cultures or time periods, then make an argument for or against those policies being put into place in our modern-day government.

- **Make a sales pitch.** In all subject areas, a sales pitch increases the idea that our students can create and run their own businesses instead of working for someone else. This idea is not mentioned nearly enough in many of our most impoverished neighborhoods.

  ► *Math:* Students can demonstrate simple math skills by integrating financial literacy into math. They can put together a pitch and consider the cost of supplies and how much income they hope to make. Then, in the upper grades, students can scale up the operation.

  ► *Geography:* Students can demonstrate their understanding of a geographic location by choosing an appropriate item to sell and determining how they would market it to that location and culture.

▶ *Language arts:* Students could work on persuasive writing in a way that is more connected to the real world than the traditional "Should schools require uniforms?" Students could even write a persuasive essay in the form of a script for a commercial.

- **Create a TikTok-style video.** In her book *Culturally Responsive Teaching and the Brain,* Zaretta Hammond argues that it is essential for engaging instruction to be rooted in youth culture. That is not to say teachers must be fluent in youth speak or up to date with all the trends. They should, however, have a finger on the pulse of what engages young people outside the walls of the school building. If you ask students to create a short video covering the unit's content, it could result in an awesome demonstration of student knowledge.

  ▶ *Social studies:* Students can create an informational, "Did you know?" style of video that would be similar to an essay on a topic. The difference is that it could include transitions, feature multiple students on camera, and include other forms of media that connect to the content. For example, if the students were making a video about the transition from the Civil Rights Movement of the early 1960s to the Black Power Movement of the late '60s and early '70s, the students could use James Brown's pro-Black anthem "Say It Loud (I'm Black and I'm Proud)."

  ▶ *Science:* Students can make a video while performing an engaging experiment or record someone else doing the experiment and narrate what is happening according to what they learned in the unit. It's like citing someone else's work when writing a paper. Students can give credit to the person doing the experiment and still share the learning as their own.

> ► *Language:* For students learning a second language, making videos has long been an assessment approach. One reason is that acquiring a language is so much more than the ability to match vocabulary words or even produce writing in a second language. It includes producing the language in oral communication as well. Again, students could use the creativity of the platform and mix it with the language content.

- **Tell a story (Storify).** As mentioned in Hack 1, collectivist cultures tell stories. Research from the field of neurology demonstrates that the human brain is wired for stories. MRIs done while a person is listening to a story show that the parts of the brain associated with the actions taken by the story's character light up for the listener. A story makes the brain feel as though it is participating in these actions. This truth is part of what makes this strategy a great form of assessment. Creating a story to tell will help the brain remember the content.

  > ► *Math:* A simple form of this idea is the age-old hungry gator. For generations, math teachers have taught greater than/less than by describing the signs as an alligator's mouth. The alligator always wants to eat a bigger number. This strategy can be used elsewhere, too. For the steps of long division, students could write a story demonstrating their understanding of the process.

> ▶ *Science:* Students can write a story that features the life cycle of a plant or an animal. An example of this approach is the award-winning children's book by Eric Carle, *The Very Hungry Caterpillar*.

> ▶ *Geography:* Storytelling can be used for a technical description in any subject, including geography. When students use stories to describe the formation of the mountains or retell a cultural story from a certain place in the world, they demonstrate their learning.

- **Create a game.** A high cognitive demand is required to play role-playing games. Creating a game would also require high-level thinking. Thinking through the rules of the game is a way for students to demonstrate their knowledge and understanding of the content. As the students create the games, allow them to play one another's games.

  > ▶ *Language arts:* Students can create a board game based on the book they read as a small group. The game setting would be demonstrated in the design of the board game and the rules. The characters could be playable or simply move the story along. In this way, students can show their understanding of the literature.

  > ▶ *Math:* Students can create a game in which they must get basic computational questions correct. Moreover, they could create a game with various word problems by drawing different cards and demonstrating a high level of understanding of the content.

▶ *Biology:* Students could create a game displaying their understanding of the scientific process of genetic reproduction. They could use a Punnett square to determine which gene will be passed on.

WHAT *YOU* CAN DO TOMORROW

Often, assessments are pre-selected by the district based on past practice or the set curriculum. While this is important for comparing data across the buildings, it does not represent the teacher's knowledge of the students in the classroom. The teacher may know about students' interests and be looking to introduce them into the unit. The singular mode of assessment does not meet the needs of each student. Instead, teachers can adjust their assessments, whether summative or formative, for maximum engagement by all students, including those failing tests and essays. You can implement these ideas immediately.

- **Consider your students' interests, strengths, and weaknesses when designing an assessment.**
  Ensure you know what your students like and dislike, both generally and specifically, where possible. Understand your students' skills and consider them as you design activities. Remember that test taking and essay writing are strengths for some but weaknesses for others. If your purpose is to measure student competence on the standard, don't let their weaknesses get in the way of assessing.

- **Review the standards and be clear about what they are asking for.** To have an accurate assessment, it is necessary to understand what is being assessed. The educator must clearly understand the success criteria for each standard being assessed. It is recommended that teachers review a unit's standards before teaching it, as it helps the educator begin with the end in mind. It also helps keep the teacher's mind focused on what to measure rather than just choosing a cool project they like.

- **Keep the same rubric but change the performance task.** If your district has rubrics for every measure of student learning, it is a step ahead of others. One way to ensure the data reviewed at the district level remains the same is to use the same rubrics to assess certain math exams and written pieces. As long as the rubrics are based on the standards, they can still be used, even if the new task includes more than completing a piece of paper or writing an essay.

- **Work on one assessment at a time.** When a high-quality teacher gets excited about assessing and how it can impact instructional practice, the teacher may be tempted to take on more work than is bearable. Slow and steady wins the race. Take on one assessment, reflect, improve, and then move on to the next.

- **Be clear and concise in your instructions for the new task.** If students have never been asked to do appraisals like those described in this Hack, they might find it intimidating. Be as clear as possible in the verbiage used to describe the task. Students will want to know that they can be the most successful on any given assignment. It is of utmost importance that students understand the criteria for successful completion of the assessment.

A BLUEPRINT FOR FULL IMPLEMENTATION

To effectively implement non-traditional assessments in the classroom, educators must first adopt a comprehensive and flexible assessment blueprint. It begins with identifying clear instructional objectives aligned with learning outcomes that form the foundation for all assessment activities. The blueprint should include various authentic assessment methods, such as portfolios, self-assessments, peer evaluations, project-based learning, and performance tasks allowing students to demonstrate their knowledge and skills in real-world contexts. Here are a few steps to implement this Hack.

STEP 1: Select an assessment for an upcoming unit.

When preparing to teach a unit of study, start with the end in mind. It is an excellent practice to begin with a review of the unit's final assessment. However, perhaps the form of the unit assessment is mandated by the district curriculum team. The concept of trading out an essay or test can be done for a formative assessment as well. When selecting an assessment, consider the depth of thought that the assessment allows.

STEP 2: Review the assessment and reflect on what students need to know, understand, or be able to do.

Once you have selected the assessment, it is time to dive deep into what it asks students to do. What exactly does it want students to know, understand, and be able to do? You can find this information by stepping back from the assessment and looking at the standards connected to the overarching standard. A deep study of the standards, breaking them down into comprehensible, smaller statements, will help ensure that students will continue to meet those standards, even if the assessment is in another format. Additionally, many assessments, particularly essays, already have rubrics for how the end products should be assessed. It's another area to think about what the student needs to know.

> WE MUST BE SURE THAT LEARNING HAPPENS FOR ALL STUDENTS, ESPECIALLY OUR STUDENTS WHO MIGHT OTHERWISE STRUGGLE WITH ESSAY AND TEST FORMATS.

One additional piece to include in your reflection is about the skills students need to complete this learning task in a format other than an essay or test. If students will be asked to work in small groups or with technology, other aspects will need to be included in the instruction and assessment.

STEP 3: Based on what you know about your students and their language needs, convert the assessment to a non-traditional format.

We have many considerations about our students regarding converting an assessment from a test or essay into a more collaborative and student-centered assessment. They include your students' ages, the time of year, their general progress with certain academic skills, their ability to work independently in small groups, and the available staff to help in your room. Also consider their linguistic background and proficiency with both comprehending and producing the language of instruction. A critical component is student interests. What do your students like? What do you hear them talking about during social time? What do your students want to do when they grow up? How can you connect them to career ideas they have not been exposed to?

Students should be centered on **what** they will produce and **how** they will produce it. Recognize that while some students may be interested in social media trends, others have no connection to them. Some are intrigued by Japanese animation, which Americans commonly refer to as anime, while others are more into classic TV sitcoms. Again, students may be artists, musicians, or poets. It is unlikely that in one assessment, all students will be able to express themselves in their preferred method, but it's worth considering.

Ultimately, the assessment must accomplish the goal of assessing student learning, and this is where it becomes important that student learning is still centered. One challenge of this type of assignment is that it includes a risk of the assignment being more about fun and less about learning. When this happens, it hurts our most at-risk students. We must be sure that learning happens for all students, especially our students who might otherwise struggle with essay and test formats. Our hope in providing multiple formats is that students will take what they've learned and be able to show an analysis of the information and synthesize something new. The assignment must provide an opportunity for each student to demonstrate knowledge and understanding of the content.

STEP 4: Adapt instruction to include all the essential skills needed for the assessment.

Once the assessment has been adapted to include the interests and strengths of the diverse students in the classroom, think about what instruction you must also adapt. Instruction is given differently if the only expectation is that students memorize it long enough to put it back on paper in a test format. If, however, the purpose of the assessment is now to show analysis and synthesis, the lessons must include opportunities for students to grapple with complex concepts and flex their brains in a way that will prepare them for the assessment. For example, if students will need to set up a business account to show incoming and outgoing payments to demonstrate their understanding of two- and three-digit addition and subtraction, it would be necessary to include models of that higher-level thinking in the unit of instruction.

Additionally, if you ask students to produce a project using a certain technology platform, then they need to learn about how to use that platform. You can apply this same idea to working in groups. When done well, group work is structured and features students being able to share responsibilities through defined roles. We have already discussed the importance of collaborative work in collectivist cultures. Now, we are noting that in the K–12 school system, we are still dealing with children and ultimately humans who may, on occasion, try to do as little as possible. Teaching students how to work in a group is an essential part of success in alternative assessment formats.

STEP 5: Grade the students' assessments and offer specific, actionable feedback.

Some controversy exists around how grades should work for a group project. The final product, which is the work of the group as a whole, should have some bearing on the "grade." After all, the rubric for assessing the assignment will be based, at least partially, on the outcome. However, it is incredibly important that the crux of the assessment results in specific, actionable feedback for each student.

Specific, actionable feedback is essential for student success. It helps them understand what they are doing well and where they need to improve. It also gives them the information they need to make changes and improve their work. Keep the following key ideas in mind when providing feedback to students.

- **Give specific feedback.** General feedback, such as "good job" or "you need to improve," is not helpful. Students need to know exactly what they are doing well and what they need to work on. For students also learning SAE, explicit feedback eases the cognitive load of trying to learn both language and content.

- **Give actionable feedback.** Students need to know what they can do to improve their work. Telling them they need to "improve their writing" is not helpful. They need to know specific areas where they can improve their writing, such as using more evidence to support their claims or using more specific language.

- **Give timely feedback.** Students need to receive feedback on their work as soon as possible so they can make changes and improvements.

- **Give positive and constructive feedback.** Students need to feel that they are capable of improving their work. Focus your feedback on helping students improve, not on criticizing them.

STEP 6: Reflect on the assessment as a learning community that includes your colleagues and students.

Education is based on a continuous improvement model, and a necessary component of it is reflection. A valuable step in the process is to reflect on what went well and what improvements could be made to the assessment and the instruction that preceded it.

Reflecting with students values them as partners in the teaching and learning process. Reflection with students could be a whole-class discussion after completing the assignment, or it might include a feedback form for their classmates if the project requires a presentation. It could also be as simple as a survey for students to give feedback to the teacher on the unit as a whole and on the assessment in particular. Note that for students who are used to writing essays and taking tests, these types of assessments may be seen as more challenging and too much work. It is okay to receive that feedback and consider where a test or essay can play a role in the classroom.

Reflecting with other teachers is another crucial step, especially if there is a mix of those who used the adapted assessment and those who did not. This reflection allows for data-driven discussions about the effectiveness of the assessments. Discuss how many students met the standards assessed in the unit. Teachers could share student work samples of the final products. As part of the data analysis, consider how your students from linguistically diverse backgrounds performed. This consideration will help you respond to the specific needs of that group of students based on the data. Again, with improvement in mind, teachers can share the opportunities for improvement with each other.

OVERCOMING PUSHBACK

Innovative education requires us to pivot from the familiar; hence, we understand the hesitation about non-traditional assessments and the concerns about objectivity and preparation for standardized tests. However, these dynamic assessment methods cultivate critical thinking, problem-solving, and application-based understanding—crucial elements of real-world success. Here are a few common concerns about this Hack and how to address them.

An assessment like this will be too hard for my students. Unfortunately, the students who need the most academic engagement and challenge often receive the least. The types of projects described here are often reserved for students in the gifted and talented classes. However, students who fall behind due to various life challenges are the ones who need activities that will engage them in real learning. Students who struggle are more likely to tune out when situations get hard, so it's essential to offer an activity that grabs their attention. Additionally, students can grow by using their brains in ways they did not know they could. These assessments ask students to think outside of their usual comfort zone. Our culturally and linguistically diverse students, often viewed as struggling, benefit from opportunities to process their learning through talking. These assessments center collaboration and communication.

These types of assessments have too much subjectivity in the grading process. While multiple-choice tests tend to remove the subjectivity from the grading process, it could also be said that their absence is part of the challenge of using tests. There is no room for students to show some level of understanding. The traditional test only allows for one letter to be chosen or one answer to be given. The Common Core State Standards, if those are what your state uses, are rooted in a higher level of rigor than simply knowing information and being able to reproduce it on a test.

Of course, we could also make this argument about too much subjectivity regarding the writing of an essay. The answer to this criticism with the essay is the same as with these projects: create a well-designed rubric. Teachers and students must clearly understand what is being asked of them on the assessment. One way is to review the rubric as a teaching team. Also, review the rubric with students before the unit, during the unit, and after the assessment. A clear, well-written rubric helps remove the subjectivity that makes grading non-traditional assessments a challenge.

Non-traditional assessments don't prepare our students for state testing or other standardized tests. It's an inaccurate idea that assessment formats other than tests and essays do not prepare students for standardized tests. It only requires us to look through the practice questions of the Northwest Evaluation Association's (NWEA) MAP tests or a state test. Out of familiarity, we will reference the Illinois Assessment of Readiness. The IAR is an assessment that features multi-step questions for both math and language arts. The test asks students to be able to read one passage and, yes, answer direct comprehension questions. But it also asks students to answer questions about what they can ascertain from the text. It includes questions about the use of vocabulary.

The point is that the skills students should have learned are tested through opportunities for application. On the math assessment, the math problems build on one another, where students need to have correct information on one problem to effectively do the next part of the problem correctly. The complexity of state tests and MAP tests means students are asked to do more than simply know the content.

Moreover, the non-traditional assessments discussed in this Hack also help students move what they are learning from short-term to long-term memory. When students can process the information through collaborative conversation, it is more likely to stick. When students must take the information and apply it in a situation that includes the use of knowledge previously held, they are more likely to retain it. The more students can work new learning into their old schemas, the more likely they will remember the new learning. This, again, is necessary for optimal performance on the standardized assessments that are part of our educational system.

THE HACK IN ACTION

The following story is told by Maurice McDavid.

For me, this Hack is personal. In my first year teaching, I taught four sections of eighth-grade social studies. The content was American history from 1860 through the 1960s. We did not cover the Civil War, as it was covered in seventh grade. Instead, we started with the Industrial Revolution of the 1860s. We talked about the great American businessmen of the late nineteenth century and their questionable business practices. We talked about the beginnings of American imperialism. We discussed the four presidents of the Progressive Era at the turn of the twentieth century. I don't know about you, but all this history is riveting to me. However, by the time we made it to our final unit, I realized that for my students, there was no continuity in what I was teaching them.

They were enthralled by the stories I told of exciting details in each unit, and then they took a test and let that information go. They enjoyed the learning and activities from each unit; however, they seemed unable to understand how the reckless spending of the Roaring Twenties played a role in the fallout of the Depression. They could name who was on what side in World War II but could not explain how the spending on the war helped to end the Depression. And while they could tell you about Levittowns and the development of the suburbs, they did not see how those housing styles had spawned from the GI Bill handed out after the end of the War. While students who grew up speaking SAE fared better than students from more varied linguistic backgrounds, it was not the most effective learning experience for any students.

As we approached the unit on the 1960s, I talked with my eighth-grade counterpart who taught social studies on the other team. We discussed what the school had traditionally done to assess this unit. She explained that there was a traditional test, but it was not always given because we were often up against the end of the year, and sometimes, it was skipped over or replaced with a short essay. A positive outcome of the conversation was that I could try a different approach to assessing the 1960s unit. And that is precisely what I did.

I took the unit standards and set out to create an assessment to allow students to take what they had learned up to that point in the year and put it into practice. The basic premise of the unit was that we would become experts on this decade that altered the fabric of our country. We would make a documentary about the 1960s.

There was an order to the chaos that would commence over the length of this unit. First, each of my history sections would have one of four available topics. The four topics were: Civil Rights, American Politics, Pop Culture, and Science and Technology. Once the classes had chosen their topics, the students within each class had to choose an area in which they would contribute to the documentary. They could choose from images, interviews, videos, and primary source documents. The students in each group had specific tasks to accomplish. To tie it all together, the students had to point to something from another historical period that contributed to the reality of the 1960s that they were learning about.

The result was more than I could have hoped for. To be clear, it was not perfect. It was also not without a headache. The students in the first group produced a thirty-minute documentary about America in the 1960s. Each group made a connection from a previous period to what was happening in the 1960s. They had incredible conversations with community elders about their experiences living during that time. One amazing aspect was the leadership of students who were struggling readers or from diverse linguistic backgrounds who had great ideas to share as they wrote their scripts for the voiceover portions of the video. In the following year, I added specific jobs to hold all students accountable for contributing and demonstrating their individual learning. Again, students selected their roles so they could work to their strengths, linguistic and otherwise.

One pleasure of continuing to live in the community where I started my career is that I get to run into former students. When these occurrences happen and we begin to reminisce on those eighth-grade days, we often come to this unit of study. Now, there could be several reasons for that. The 1960s held similarities to the time the students were living, and the '60s were an incredible time full of action. However, I sincerely believe that it is because they were given a different way to engage in learning and demonstrate what they had learned.

The simplicity of Hack 4 makes it one of the most easily actionable Hacks in this book. Here are ways you can ACT on this learning.

Actions:

- Review your current unit of study to see how learning is analyzed in both formative and summative methods.

- Read or re-read the standards to be assessed in your current unit of study. Discuss them with a teammate, focusing on what students are expected to know and be able to do. Talk about whether the current assessment allows students to demonstrate their knowledge and skills according to the standards.

Consider:

- How diverse are your students (racially, culturally, linguistically, and ability-wise)? Does the current assessment meet the needs of all your students?

- How can you use artificial intelligence to help create new assignments to better appraise your students' learning?

Turning Point:

- Amid a national literacy crisis that includes a high number of struggling readers, we are also seeing US public schools hit an all-time high percentage of students of color. As schools face the challenges of increasing diversification, one element of teaching must take place. We must ensure that we are assessing students' actual skills that we are teaching them. We want to know what students know and what they do not know. A struggling reader may be unable to read all the words on a traditional science test but may still understand the ideas and concepts taught in the science unit. We must give students an opportunity to shine beyond their struggles while we work to fill in the gaps.

HACK
5

BUILD A BRIDGE
Be Intentional About Two-Way Communication with Students' Families

Communication is only effective when we communicate in
a way that is meaningful to the recipient, not ourselves.
— RICH SIMMONDS, AUTHOR

THE PROBLEM: HOME-TO-SCHOOL COMMUNICATION IS DOMINATED BY SCHOOLS

*I*MAGINE HAVING DONE a job for five years and then being invited to meetings several times a year where people talk to you about how to do your job better. This scenario is the experience of a kindergarten parent who has managed to raise a child for about five years, then is invited to a school building where the staff tells them what to feed the child, what time the child should go to bed, and what the child should and should not watch. It is easy to see how the family connection to schools dwindles by the time students hit middle school.

Experts in the preschool years understand that parents or guardians are the child's first teachers. Schools do not, as a whole, tap into this resource enough. After a series of parent conferences and other events like literacy nights, parents often disconnect from the school, viewing the events as opportunities for the school to preach their "gospel" of research-based strategies and parenting approaches. It is hard to form a true partnership without a sense of equality when parents perceive an imbalance in the relationship between school officials and themselves as parents.

STAFF OFTEN MAKE AN UNSPOKEN ASSUMPTION THAT PARENTS WHO DO NOT COMMUNICATE IN THE WAY THE SCHOOL WANTS THEM TO DO NOT CARE ABOUT THEIR CHILD'S EDUCATION.

In some cases, cultural norms add to the complexity. For example, in parts of the Latino community, there is the idea that teachers and administrators are *bien educado*. This expression translates to "well-educated" and represents the idea that teachers know what is best and that parents should not question the actions and decisions of school staff. This thinking, too, can inhibit efforts to build a true partnership with parents.

In other cases, the parents may have had poor experiences with schools when they were students, and that impacted their viewpoints of the schools their children attend, resulting in a sense of distrust. This lack of trust is further exacerbated when staff are prescriptive in their initial meetings with parents. Such a directive approach can feel like an attack on what parents are already doing. Many times, parents are aware that some of their parenting strategies are not as effective as they would like them to be, but they also believe they are doing the best they can. Any critique of parents' parenting practices without a relationship can feel like an attack.

Often, there is no effort to establish an actual relationship between school staff and families. A functional relationship requires that both parties are equal or close to equal participants. Unfortunately, the school's relationship with parents can cast educators as the distributors of important information and the ones on the moral high ground. Staff often make an unspoken assumption that parents who do not communicate in the way the school wants them to do not care about their child's education.

Also, the centering of the school culture does not leave room for the various home cultures represented in the school. This, in turn, further distances the families from the school. It leaves teachers and administrators feeling like the parent is the enemy, and vice versa, instead of understanding one another as team members pulling on the same side of the rope and in the same direction. A missing component of that goal is two-way communication.

In academic or behavioral reporting, two-way communication is commonly missing from schools. Take, for example, a student whose behavior in class was deemed inappropriate. Perhaps the student was sent to the administrator's office and a call home was made. It is likely that the administrator will report to the family what happened and how it will be dealt with at school. The parent responds that they will talk to the child that evening. There is no inquisitiveness about how the parent will handle it, what the parent will say to the child, or how the school can use what is done at home to help the student succeed at school. However, these inquiries are an absolute must if the parents and the school intend to work together in the student's best interests.

The lack of two-way communication is, perhaps, most pronounced in our culturally and linguistically diverse families' relationships with the school. On occasion, it may be as surface-level as a language barrier. Many schools have what are called low-incidence languages represented in their buildings. These are languages that exist in the school with so few students that there is no legal requirement to have a staff member who speaks that language. This situation creates a literal language barrier. The language or languages spoken and written by the school do not match the language of the family. It's a real problem, and it's not the only way culturally and linguistically diverse families are left out of the loop.

Further concerns exist about two-way communication because of the *language of schools*. The *language of schools* is the language many educators speak and expect people to understand. It may sometimes be called educational jargon, but it is a language most often understood by those with the social capital necessary to learn the language. It is the language of advocacy, standing up against mistreatment, and talking to educators as equals. The fact that educators know this language gap exists means they ought to do something about it.

THE HACK: BUILD A BRIDGE

For full transparency, this Hack is a broad statement. However, it is one of the most powerful actions that can be taken in a school to help support a strong school culture and student academic progress. Be **intentional**. Intentionality requires that educators are calculated and willful about their steps. They decide, often ahead of time, to do certain things and to avoid doing other things. Communication should be **two-way**, meaning that educators are looking to hear from students' families as much or more than they are looking to share information with them. Two-way communication invites and encourages parents, guardians, and even community members to participate in the educational team supporting the work in our schools.

We will offer specific ideas about what this looks like in practice. We also want to establish that this practice can impact our work in major ways.

To elaborate, we believe two-way communication is critical for countless reasons. First, schools owe it to parents to communicate about the well-being of their child. Parents want to know and deserve to know if their student struggles in any facet of the schoolwork. Parents also should know if their child is experiencing success and how the school is helping to ensure the continuation of that success.

Second, parents have information about the whole of life and the immediate moments of life that should impact the way teachers interact with students. Parents have information to share about the loss of the child's parent some years ago or last year. Parents might share information about their child's hesitancy toward mathematics due to difficulty reading word problems. Parents could share that their student tends to talk in class when they are not engaged and has historically completed their work quickly. Some of these ideas are ones that a teacher may discover throughout the year, and others are such that teachers may never find out unless communication comes from the parent.

Third, two-way communication again promotes the idea that the educator and parent or guardian are a team. This is an important step early in any school year. It means that if the teachers must deliver challenging news to families, they already have a positive relationship that allows families to receive the information with less confrontation. Parents might think, "I know they have in mind what's best for my child." Finally, intentional two-way communication shows families that they are equals in the education process. They can make calls about their students. They can advocate for a change in programming. They can ask for more details about a graded assignment. These conversations are imperative if a family is to be a part of creating success for the student.

What this Hack looks like could show up in many different ways. Schools can practice two-way communication with parents by:

- **Providing multiple channels of communication.**
  Schools can make it easy for parents to communicate
  with teachers and administrators by including channels
  like email, phone calls, text messages, and online portals. An awesome feature of many digital portals is that
  they automatically translate the communication to the
  home language registered in the student information
  system. This is one way schools can break the language
  barrier with ease.

- **Being responsive to parent feedback.** When parents
  reach out to the school, they should expect a timely and
  helpful response. From front office staff to administration
  to teaching staff, there should be a response to parent
  feedback. It must be valued as the voice of the "cus-
  tomer." Every parent's voice matters, not only those who
  are classroom volunteers. Schools should also make it
  easy for parents to provide feedback on school programs
  and policies, and school committees play a key role.

- **Sharing information about student progress.** Schools
  can inform parents about their child's academic progress, including grades, attendance, and behavior. Schools
  can also provide opportunities for parents to meet with
  teachers to discuss their child's progress. During these
  conferences, it is ideal for parents to share information
  about what they are seeing outside of school. Additionally,
  the school staff can share simple strategies that parents
  can use at home to practice academic and social-emotional skills that students are learning in school.

- **Inviting parents to participate in school activities.**
  Schools can encourage parents to volunteer in the classroom, attend events, and serve on committees, helping

parents feel connected to the school and their child's education. As you think about inviting parents into events, find ways for parents to participate and lead events. In a traditional sense, it may be through the parent-teacher organization (PTO). However, it may be through an event where parents can share what they do for a living. One way to purposefully include all families is through a culture fair. At a culture fair, parents share parts of their culture with the rest of the community. In both the career fair and culture fair, parents get to feel like the experts. The parent perspective is vital to committees. Some states, like Illinois, require the presence of parents on certain committees, and it's a fantastic opportunity to involve a diverse group of parents in giving direct feedback and having direct input into the district's decisions.

- **Celebrating student successes.** Schools can share student successes with parents, including academic achievements, extracurricular activities, and community service. Celebrating student successes helps parents feel proud of their children and the school. We see increased parent engagement around activities like athletics, particularly at the secondary level. Another popular way to engage parents is through academic honors ceremonies. Every parent loves to hear how well their child is doing. Having parents come in large numbers to an event is an excellent time to get those parents involved in events at your school. Take time to hear from parents while they are present in your building.

- **Inviting parents to parent cafés to build relationships with each other.** A parent café is a parent event designed to build community among the parents through structured conversations. Different models can be used to operate a parent café, and the main purpose is to build parent expertise. The neat part about cafés is that ideally, a staff member is not lecturing about how parents should parent their children at home. This model allows neighborhood families with similar experiences to speak to the expertise they have developed with the school. It is awesome to watch parents learn from one another the different strategies to help support their students.

- **Surveying the parents.** Surveys are one of the easiest methods to engage parents and get their feedback. It is, of course, also the least personal. Under many circumstances, the surveys sent out by schools are anonymous. Nonetheless, they allow schools to receive feedback from a larger number of families all at once. Schools can then disaggregate the survey data by identifying factors to see trends among the different parent groups or student groups. A powerful move often skipped in the survey process is sharing the survey results with parents. This step lets parents know their feedback is being viewed and considered.

We cannot produce an exhaustive list of all the ways schools can use two-way communication, and one reason is that two-way communication can exist in all grade levels and all environments across a school district. One way to ensure this is accomplished is to create a communication plan. The plan could list the specific communication environment (such as the classroom, multi-tiered system of supports, social-emotional learning/behavioral, or whole school). It could also include the theme of the communication. Example themes are registration, parent-teacher conferences, or social-emotional screenings. Finally, it could include how you intend to receive feedback from families in response to that communication. At the classroom level, it often consists of an ask such as a physical signature, a note back, or a response via the electronic portal. Similar requests occur with small-group communications for MTSS or positive behavioral interventions and supports. As the messages are sent to the whole building, a survey might be an easier way to get a response because, again, it allows for an easier collection of large amounts of data.

WHAT *YOU* CAN DO TOMORROW

Of all the Hacks presented in this book, this one is one of the easiest to begin implementing tomorrow. The following actions and activities can increase the two-way communication with all of your families, emphasizing those who are not showing up in regular communication logs.

- **Send a communication to all parents in a classroom, requesting their help with filling out a student profile.** As for the student profile, teachers can create their own or find ideas online. Once you finalize the profile, send it home and let parents share their thoughts about their students. This profile is one way to establish a positive relationship and emphasize that the parents are their children's first teacher.

- **Invite parents to set academic or behavioral goals through academic parent-teacher teams.** APTT is a model that focuses on bridging the responsibility for student progress between school and home. Perhaps at a fall open house or after the fall benchmark assessments, have parents review their students' data. Then ask parents to set an academic goal with their students. Ideally, you could do this in person, but you could also create a form that helps explain how to set a specific, measurable, achievable, relevant, and time-bound—or SMART—goal. Share ideas for reasonably attainable goals with the families. Communicate simple, at-home strategies parents can use with their students to practice the foundational skills for the grade level. Throughout the year, check the students' performance progress by reviewing assessment data. You can find more information about APTT on our website, blackbrownbilingue.com, under Resources.

- **Host an evening for parents to collaborate with each other.** You can start planning an event like this tomorrow, whether at the building, grade-level, or classroom level. You only need childcare, food to draw people in, and great conversation prompts that start with an icebreaker. Many parents want to be more involved in school and in their children's academic lives, but they have the job of parenting. Childcare relieves that burden. Parents also need to make sure their family eats. Providing dinner takes care of that. Finally, some adults have a higher sense of social anxiety around interacting with people they do not know. Acknowledge that in the room and then explain that the goal for the evening is to bust through that anxiety and estab-lish a learning community, which is a great place to learn the *language of schools*.

- **Invite parents to volunteer.** Schools can build two-way communication by encouraging parents to vol-unteer in the classroom or at school events. This involvement will help parents get to know their child's teacher and see what is happening in the classroom.

A BLUEPRINT FOR FULL IMPLEMENTATION

Beyond a doubt, two-way communication is a practice for every educator and school leader to strive for. However, the hope or intention of two-way communication is not enough. They must develop a plan and put it into place to support this endeavor. Take the following steps and adjust them to fit your situation.

STEP 1: Assess current communication protocols.

First, review the ways communication with families is currently operating. How often and on what platforms is it happening? Consider the current methods that allow for two-way communication and evaluate how much you use them. Most schools have a system or platform that allows for two-way communication, but the true assessment is in how much it is being used to build engaged families. Just because a family responds to your message does not mean they are engaged in two-way communication. The key is that they can lead the conversation at times, too.

STEP 2: Develop goals for family engagement.

Based on the assessment of current communication, we recommend you set one to three communication goals for the school year. This step can be accomplished at the classroom, building, or district level. The complexity of the goals will be determined by where your organization is in the process of establishing two-way communication. The following example goals use the SMART goal format.

- I will have one hundred parent volunteers in the classroom setting by the end of the current school year.

- I will have a "Your Learner at Home" survey completed by a parent/guardian for 100 percent of my students by October 15 of the current school year.

- My district will host five successful district-wide parent cafés with defined success criteria by the end of the school year.

- The parent engagement score on the state-mandated school culture survey will go up 3.5 percentage points annually.

You will notice that many of these goals are related to the number of events. The goals allow for a specific, measured amount to define success. However, we also need to ensure all interactions, surveys, and parent cafés are done with fidelity. This brings us to our third step.

STEP 3: Create a plan for reaching your communication goals.

Many people set goals at the beginning of the school year, but a goal without a plan is just a wish. It is necessary to create a plan for how to accomplish two-way communication this year. It is worth the time and effort to create the plan and begin implementing it. An effective communication plan should consider these three factors: what is being communicated, when is it being communicated, and how is it being communicated.

Before we examine each factor in greater detail, remember that the word "communication" shares the same root as the word "community." It is not about simply giving information but about building community.

What is being communicated?

Author and executive coach Jim Davis says our behavior must match our goal. The communication sent to parents must match the goals we have set. While we must communicate certain topics throughout the year about field trips, evening events, and grades, we also must ensure we have a plan in place to share the messages that are important for reaching the goals we set. For example, if the goal is to get volunteers into the school building, it is paramount that we produce frequent communications asking for volunteers. The request for volunteers can be a part of every mundane communication we send. It should be in every language represented in the student body so it is inviting to everyone. Additionally, we need to provide a way for families to respond to the request or any other information in the communication. Often, that is a phone number to the main office or an electronic method of responding.

When is it being communicated?

In show business, they say timing is everything. Regarding two-way communication in the school setting, timing is also of great importance. To the extent that it is possible, let families say when is the best time to receive communication. If you're hoping for a conversation, send the message when families have the time and space to respond. We're sure you can think of a time when communication was delayed because you couldn't respond in that moment, and then you forgot to respond later. Consider a family in which the caregivers work the second shift. A message during the early evening is in the middle of their work time. Because you hope to build community with each family, it can be helpful to individualize communication times.

Another part of the "when" question is in connection to the calendar. Attempting to give families time to plan for an event is key. Communications that are a regular, guaranteed part of the year can be scheduled, and the schedule can be shared with parents so they know the cadence of communication. For example, let them know if they can expect a monthly schoolwide newsletter, a monthly learning report, and a trimester grade report every three months. If music concerts are already scheduled, send that information as a "save the date" to get the most participation.

Finally, take advantage of having parents in the building when they are there for special events. Face-to-face communication is a strong way to build lasting and impactful relationships that benefit student learning. At a well-attended event, it is impossible to have a conversation with everyone. A survey is a wonderful way to gather information from people at an event. You can create electronic surveys using various online platforms (e.g., Google Forms, SurveyMonkey) and then turn them into a QR code that participants can scan from a smartphone. Again, be sure to include the survey in the languages represented in the school building.

How is it being communicated?

A school must communicate with families in ways that are responsive to the various cultures and communities it serves. Families' levels of education, access to technology, and socioeconomic status could impact how they participate in a community. Consider that a family in which parents have not finished school themselves may be better served by a video or audio communication than a letter or text. Another scenario is one in which families travel for work. Those families may benefit from a communication that they can look at when they have the chance to slow down. Another consideration is the familiarity with the school system as a whole. In communities with high immigrant populations, the families may not be as familiar with the American school system. Communication with these families cannot work under the presupposition that they understand what "school registration" is, for example.

When communicating with families, pause and ask, "Is anyone being left out by this method of communication?" Technology is certainly a way to help close that gap. If a parent or caregiver can't make an in-person meeting, offer them the ability to join via video conferencing. Ensure there is an audio version of the communication available whenever feasible to support communication with people who are visually impaired or unable to read or write.

The three questions we just discussed and the goals we created for communication can drive the creation of a plan. The plan should be detailed enough that there are no questions about what tasks need to be completed, when they need to be completed by, and who is responsible for them.

STEP 4: Assess the effectiveness of your plan and adjust as necessary.

We all know that initial versions of plans are rarely the same ones that go into place. An important part of two-way communication is assessing whether it is actually *two-way*. When you create a plan, check its effectiveness and ensure it includes a way to respond if it is not meeting the goals. If the data is trending in the direction that the goal will not be met, hypothesize which strategy in the plan is not working. Adjust the strategy and let it get to work. Too often, schools have a set mode of communication and expect families to adjust to it. We must be willing to adjust our communication to be effective for all students and families.

OVERCOMING PUSHBACK

Communication can be challenging between two people who are face to face and want to talk. It is further complicated by the need to communicate with a whole class of students' families. Some families may seem like they are not interested in responding, leading educators to question the care and concern of caregivers, making the relationship with them oppositional. Creating a plan to improve communication takes time. We know, however, that it is incredibly worth it. As obstacles arise, here are a few ways to address them.

What about the challenge of the family that "never" responds? Undoubtedly, when trying to build strong two-way communication, you will run into the parent/guardian/family that seems like they never respond to your communications. Partner with administration, social workers, or other school resources that can help connect you to the family. When you do make that first contact, ask how they prefer to receive communication and what they feel is a reasonable time to give each other to respond. This request helps to build an alliance with the family while also holding them accountable to whatever expectations you establish collaboratively.

Creating and implementing a communication plan takes too much time. Our inflexibility regarding communication has hampered the development of positive relationships with culturally and linguistically diverse families. Building relationships with culturally and linguistically diverse families is not too much work. It is not extra work. It is *the* work. Like the research that demonstrates the powerful impact of teacher-student relationships, relationships with the home community positively influence student

> BUILDING RELATIONSHIPS WITH CULTURALLY AND LINGUISTICALLY DIVERSE FAMILIES IS NOT TOO MUCH WORK. IT IS NOT EXTRA WORK. IT IS *THE* WORK.

outcomes. Sometimes, building that relationship means slowing down in order to speed up. Building and implementing this plan will give you time back later in the school year. It allows you to build a relationship with families so that if and when challenges arise, it will not be your first time communicating with the family. Finally, the home community has so much information to offer to the classroom teacher to help the students experience the most academic and social success.

These parents aren't engaged because they don't care about school. Schools are serving organizations. That means it is our job as educators to engage families. To make the statement that families are not engaged is to say that we have not accomplished one of our goals as an organization. When we take responsibility for engaging families, we take a step in the right direction. Additional actions we can take to effectively engage families include ensuring that information can travel freely back and forth.

One reason parents do not engage with schools is that, too often, information only travels one way. In these situations, parents do not get the opportunity to offer any information but are being "preached at" about what they can do better or what they are failing to do at all. When we give parents the opportunity to feel like the experts they are about their own children, we engage them as equal partners. A way to engage parents further is to partner with them beyond their role as parents. Invite parents to serve as role models, talking about what they do for work or explaining their family's culture.

THE HACK IN ACTION

The following story is told by Maurice McDavid.

The fall of 2020 was a difficult one for all school administrators. However, I experienced an additional challenge because it was my first year as a principal in a new district. And we were in the middle of a global pandemic. While the world was encouraged to maintain at least a six-foot distance from one another, much of what was considered communication was relegated to little square boxes on a computer. Often, there were more questions than answers. I knew that communication would be a key part of my job that year, with rules and regulations changing every day. With the assistance of a more veteran administrator, I sat down and created a communication plan for the school year. It started with an introductory YouTube video in English and Spanish, the two main languages spoken in the district.

Throughout the fall, communications went out in English and Spanish via written messages and phone calls. On top of all that, I sent out a link to video announcements. Every Friday, I would do the announcements in the form of a rap video. It was time consuming and required energy, but I stuck with it. Many teachers loved it and appreciated the fun it brought to a challenging situation. I also received pushback. Some teachers viewed the videos, especially the "Freestyle Fridays," as a waste of time.

I had the benefit of seeing the results of my investment. On Mondays, I was required to host a Coffee Talk on Zoom. These chats were an opportunity for me to share news and updates and to answer any questions. Ahead of major updates, the Zoom calls were always full. Many parents commented during those calls that, although they had not worked with me in person, they felt like they knew me and could trust me. As part of my communication plan, I set a goal of averaging fifteen parents per call. By the time the district was ready to bring students back to the school building, I asked to adjust the cadence of the Zoom meetings, noticing that the parents only came in droves when big updates would be shared. The district leadership team refused to change from weekly meetings, even though the existing schedule was not effective. The data showed that the off weeks were bringing down the average attendance.

The students returned to the building after spring break, and with them came questions from families. This process went incredibly smoothly, as trust had already been built through a consistent cadence of communication, including opportunities for families to share their thoughts and ideas. Eventually, the district administrative team agreed to move the meetings to a less frequent occurrence, and I reached my communication goal. Some people argue that not a lot of learning happened during the COVID year. I disagree, since I lived through it as a principal and saw the learning firsthand. It was an incredible learning experience about the value of building and sustaining two-way communication. The efforts of that first year are still paying dividends several years later as I continue to lead.

Now it's your turn to reflect, plan, and implement your learning as you build a bridge of communication.

Actions:

- Review the number of languages spoken in your classroom or school. Ensure the communication platform you use can translate accurately back and forth between English and other languages.

- Establish a pattern of sending communication to families with certain guaranteed intervals, emphasizing your request for a response from parents.

Consider:

- Be intentional about the purpose of your communication. Are parents expected to simply consume certain information while they need to read and respond to other information?

- Remember the cultural communication norms for the various groups your school serves. Communication is more than messages sent back and forth. In what ways are you inviting parents and guardians into the conversation as equal partners with valuable ideas to add?

Turning Point:

- In Illinois, part of the "School Report Card" for institutions is impacted by how parents rate the communication of each school. It's important to note, the State Board of Education says, because schools with great communication are more ready for school improvement. Schools cannot work in isolation, only serving students between the morning school bell and the dismissal bell. We must purposefully build relationships with students and their families.

HACK
6

SEE THEIR STRENGTHS AND USE THEM

Apply an Asset-Based Pedagogy

One who enjoys finding errors will then start creating errors to find.
— CRISS JAMI, POET

THE PROBLEM: STUDENTS' STRENGTHS ARE OVERLOOKED WHEN THE FOCUS IS ON DEFICITS

*I*N ILLINOIS, WHERE we both live and serve as educators, nearly half of public school students live in poverty. Over 10 percent of the students are identified as English learners. This stat does not include the students who passed the English assessment but are still learning their new language, nor does it include those who speak an English dialect other than Standard American English. We mention this information because these are all items we tend to see as deficits. We could go on and talk about a student's family dynamics, housing or neighborhood, and behaviors toward adults in the school, and we could claim that the student has too many obstacles to overcome. We see every challenge, real or perceived, our students face, and sometimes, we use them to build a monument to why success is nearly impossible for them.

DEFICIT THINKING IS SIMPLY THE STORIES WE TELL OURSELVES TO MAKE IT OKAY FOR STUDENTS TO FAIL.

Deficit thinking typically introduces two problems. The first is that deficit thinking places the blame on the student or the student's situation. The second is that deficit thinking tends to make the teacher a powerless bystander in the situation. Both ideas are untrue in a classroom that is committed to equity for all students. When we say, "That student's mother works all the time and does not read with him, so of course, he is behind in reading," we are placing responsibility for the lack of reading growth on the student's circumstance. The inverse of that statement would be, "That boy reads really well because his mother is a stay-at-home mom and works with him all the time." Implied in both of those statements is that the teacher does not play a role in moving learning forward for students. Thus, deficit thinking is not only focused on the deficit of students but also of educators. It's not a small problem; it is a large social justice problem. (For more about this topic, see the book *Hacking Deficit Thinking: 8 Reframes That Will Change the Way You Think About Strength-based Practices and Equity in Schools* by Byron McClure and Kelsie Reed.)

The impact of deficit thinking harms students. When teachers have a deficit-based pedagogy, students suffer negative side effects. The issues may include:

- Students have less confidence in themselves academically and socially.

- Students are more likely to report that they do not like school.

- Students do not perform as well on assessments or other classwork.

- Teachers feel less responsibility to help these students succeed.

Unfortunately, this deficit thinking often falls along the lines of race, socioeconomic status, ability, and, you guessed it, linguistic comprehension centering SAE. Students of color enter classrooms in America carrying the burden of our recent educational history. The standardized testing movement has promoted the idea of an achievement gap. Thus, students of color may enter the classroom already being perceived as those who will need extra help and less likely to be successful. Even when teachers approach these students with empathy, it can turn into deficit thinking and lowered expectations.

This teacher behavior is repeated for both students living in poverty and students receiving support through special education. Teachers and administrators alike will disaggregate data, looking at the findings of students with special needs and excusing lower performance because the students have Individualized Education Plans (IEPs). Deficit thinking is simply the stories we tell ourselves to make it okay for students to fail. The language we use to discuss many students does not include the whole picture.

THE HACK: SEE THEIR STRENGTHS AND USE THEM

We miss the many strengths our students bring into the classroom. For Black children growing up in neighborhoods systemically impacted by a disproportionate amount of violence and poverty, they must demonstrate grit and resilience by coming to school every day. For those whose families have gone through the long process of seeking asylum in the United States, they are very familiar with persistence. For students who already read in one language, their ability to learn to read in English will be rooted in the strength that they are already readers. For those who already speak two languages, the fact that English is not one of them is not a deficit but an opportunity to become trilingual. We must understand that we and our students are capable of so much. We must look past deficits and focus on assets.

The foundation of this Hack is that every student has strengths, value, and potential. From there, we can move to finding the strengths of our students and using them to build up our students as independent, engaged, lifelong learners. When we understand our students' strengths, we can modify our lessons to ensure the information is disseminated and received, processed, and stored. Asset-based pedagogies do not view students as blank slates ready to be filled up but instead acknowledge their lived experiences, aiming to build on their base knowledge and understanding. This process requires teachers to take the time to learn about their students, their communities, and the multiple cultures represented in the classroom. We must then turn the knowledge we gain about our students into intentional decisions about our instructional practices.

Ultimately, an asset-based approach to teaching and learning requires self-reflection on the part of the educator. If students are not successful in the classroom, we must not fall back on the deficit mindset and espouse the many roadblocks students face to explain their performance. Instead, we must see what else we can learn—about the students and our practices—to come back the next week and try a different approach. Another aspect of the foundation of this Hack is that every educator has value, strengths, and the potential to positively impact every student the educator works with.

Asset-based pedagogies have been referred to as culturally responsive, culturally relevant, or even culturally sustaining teaching. We bring to the forefront an additional idea of linguistically responsive pedagogy that considers the impact of the languages students are bringing to school. Beyond that, many educators refer to a student's funds of knowledge. While distinctions exist between these ideas at the research level, one detail is true of all of them. The positive results are based on centering the students and their backgrounds, with an intense focus on student achievement.

One of the most important reasons this Hack is worth the time is that it is about the success of all students. It is where we can light a fire within ourselves to further the intentional, ongoing conversation about equity in schools and the linguistic diversity of our students. It is an open acknowledgment that the way we have always "done school" cannot continue to be the way we "do school" because it is not producing success uniformly for all students. The danger of all the conversations and different ways of talking about asset-based pedagogies is that all we will do is talk.

Being an asset-based educator requires action. It could be simple at first. Survey the students and families, asking them to identify their interests, strengths, and learning styles. (This topic could be covered in the survey referenced in Hack 2.) Attend a lunch or cultural event in the community you serve. Connect the standards and content of your lessons to the lives and communities of the students in front of you in authentic ways. Learn about the languages students speak, the religions they practice, and the holidays they celebrate. However, your learning must turn into instructional design.

The crux of this Hack is to take what you learn about your students and integrate it into the planning and implementation of instruction. If storytelling is key to the cultures in your classroom, find ways to present information in story form. Learn and use words and ideas from the language and culture of your students. For example, when discussing investment, a teacher may talk about a *tanda*, a concept many students from Latin America would be familiar with. For readers unfamiliar with it, a *tanda* is an informal, community-based way to gather a large chunk of money. Families, friends, and coworkers will enter into an agreement in which they all put an agreed-upon amount of money into a pot each month, and a different person gets it and can use it to make larger purchases.

No matter the grade level or the content, knowing your students' strengths produces better outcomes in student learning. We understand this and are often already implementing this idea regarding academics. A teacher might assess a kindergarten student at the beginning of the year to better understand how many letters the student can identify. The outcome of that assessment can be viewed either through the lens of the number of letters the student *doesn't* know or the number of letters the student *does* know. Additionally, we can celebrate the idea that the student already knows many numbers and is likely to learn letters with ease because they have a strength in symbol recognition.

This practice is also applicable in the high school math classroom, though it is perhaps one of the most difficult places to remember these pedagogies because, in the minds of many math teachers, math is just math. Unfortunately, we also know that students are failing math in droves. How do we address students' disengagement with math? We show students that they have strengths that are applicable in math. We adjust our instruction to match those strengths, and build from there. Success is possible for all students in all subjects when we figure out how to identify and build on their strengths.

WHAT *YOU* CAN DO TOMORROW

The next time you walk into your classroom, we sincerely hope you will be ready to implement asset-based pedagogies. These pedagogies require skills you must practice. They require additional energy and effort. You will not master them in one day, but you can take action tomorrow that will increase the likelihood that your students of color, your language learners, and your otherwise marginalized students will see increased success in school and in their lives outside of school.

- **Actively learn about the community you serve.** The relevance of the content you teach in your classroom is different depending on the community where you are teaching. Learn about the community you serve. You can take many avenues to learn more about your community. Attend events, patronize local shops, and meet and talk with established community members. Of course, it is not sufficient to simply take in this knowledge; we must purposefully integrate this new learning into our instruction. For example, if a factory is a major employer in the community, find ways that your content connects to the various employment opportunities the plant offers. If there is a known problem in the community, integrate opportunities in the curriculum to help solve that problem.

- **Survey your students and their families to learn about their backgrounds.** In our global society, a classroom may contain students from multiple countries who speak multiple languages. It is valuable to learn about each individual student, including details about their home lives. Learning about the cultural norms of students helps in many ways. In Hack 7, you will learn about how it can help clarify communication to avoid unnecessary student discipline, but it also impacts how students learn. Thinking about how new information is communicated at home can help establish communication routines in the school. Ask students and their parents to describe the strengths of the student to give teachers a great place to start before doing further analysis to discover additional strengths the student possesses. If a student has lived in another country or another part of the country, it can be an asset when talking about geography, climate, or politics. Multiple perspectives are key in a classroom when teaching critical thinking.

- **Be intentional about the way you talk about your students.** The way we talk about our students can impact their learning outcomes. We must carefully acknowledge and encourage our students based on their strengths. When giving assessment feedback to students, acknowledge what they did well. When pointing out the areas they need to work on, note a quality they possess that makes you confident they can and will make the improvements. Occasionally, educators engage in negative talk about students or families they serve. Typically, it is not ill-willed, but it is powerful, nonetheless. Challenge yourself to keep the strengths of your students and their families at the forefront of your mind.

A BLUEPRINT FOR FULL IMPLEMENTATION

Let us emphasize it again: *every* student has strengths. Effective instruction requires that we find those strengths and use them to build strong academic communities. Language plays a key role in this area. As you work through each step, communication will help propel you forward.

SUCCESS IS POSSIBLE FOR ALL STUDENTS IN ALL SUBJECTS WHEN WE FIGURE OUT HOW TO IDENTIFY AND BUILD ON THEIR STRENGTHS.

STEP 1: **Learn as much as you can about your students with your students.**

Despite the simplistic views often presented by political commentators, the nature of human beings is remarkably intricate and multifaceted. None of the student groups represented in our classrooms are monoliths. There is no one kind of language learner, or Black male student, or Latina student. Instead, we must take our students' heritages, languages, countries of origin, and other known identities and add the specific details of the students' lives. The stories of two immigrant families may share similarities but will be shaped by the countries of origin and even the positions of the families in their home nations. Perhaps they were refugees. Perhaps they were business owners whose shop closed due to foreign competition. Each student has a different story, and teachers who want to implement this Hack must learn each story to the best of their abilities.

We understand this is a challenging task at whatever grade level you teach. In elementary schools, the students cannot always express themselves well enough to tell their stories. At the high school level, you face other challenges. Some students have learned to cope with trauma by keeping themselves closed off and thus are unwilling to share their stories. An additional challenge at the middle and high school levels is the sheer number of students coming into your classroom and the short time you spend with them each day. However, through intentional and systematic efforts, it can happen. Here are a few ideas for getting to know your students.

- **Parent/student surveys:** As mentioned earlier, a survey is valuable for gathering information from your students and their families. Additionally, the data is organized as it comes in, if given electronically. Students may be more willing to share information in this way than through conversations.

- **Classroom conversations:** Giving students time to talk to one another and you helps to increase student engagement and learning. It also enables you to learn more about your students. Students often share more than they know as they talk about themselves in relation to the content.

- **Teacher/student journals:** Encourage students to write using classroom journals. You can provide prompts or have them do a free write. Consider using the journal as a place where students can reflect on their learning, giving you insight on how they feel about their learning progress.

Keeping up with all this student information is paramount. At the secondary level, it will be especially necessary to have organized information and to set up particular intervals at which you will review the information to keep it fresh. As you do so, ask yourself about the strengths of your students.

Another component of getting to know your students is getting to know the community in which they live. Attending sports or theater events at the school is a great way to see the pride placed in the community. Another great opportunity exists in our social media landscape by joining online groups to discover what is happening in the community. Another option is to become involved in local government. Understanding how the city's demographics have changed or are changing can provide ideas for how you can help your students thrive in the face of community responses. Knowing the community will support your efforts to get to know the kids.

STEP 2: Plan lessons with *your* students in mind.

Every year, a new group of students walks into our schools and classrooms. Even if a teacher rolls up a grade level with their students or has students again for a different class, they must acknowledge that students grow and change. Gone are the days when the same lesson can be taught every fall for thirty years (if those days ever existed). Today, we must plan lessons for the students sitting in front of us, and we must plan with their strengths and needs in mind. We recognize that this may seem like a basic concept, but we also all have a colleague who has not adjusted their lesson plans since 1993, when their students were all homogeneous. Today, we know better, so we must do better.

As you plan your lessons, consider what you have learned about your students. Work purposefully to integrate what you have learned into the lesson plans. This integration may include the topics you choose to highlight. If you know that farming is a particularly strong part of the community for some of your students, use farming as part of the lens for a lesson. In a deeper sense, if you know that you have students who thrive during group activities, include collaborative learning opportunities in your lesson plans.

What worked to move learning forward for students even last year may need to be adjusted to suit the students who are now present in your classroom. Beyond interests and topics, your instructional strategies may need to change based on what you have learned about your students. Students who are strong, independent readers may be able to read an article independently in preparation for a class discussion. Students who are stronger auditory processors may need to read the article aloud in small groups before the classroom discussion.

If the lesson objective is the critical analysis of an article, then it does not matter whether the students can read it independently. We can assign the reading of the article according to the students' strengths, and then the critical analysis is accessible for all. In a similar sense, students who are already reading in Spanish may be able to read an article in Spanish and analyze that article. They can then speak with someone who reads an article in English and compare and contrast as part of the analysis. This process allows Spanish-speaking students to practice their skill in using their assets while continuing to improve their English.

STEP 3: Lead your learners in assessing the learning.

A critical step in using an asset-based approach to teaching and learning revolves around assessments. Assessments should include at least two parts. Students should be involved in assessing themselves, and the teacher should give actionable feedback. In both parts, the assessment can be framed through the lens of students' assets.

- *Student self-assessment*: Self-assessment is an ideal opportunity to show students their strengths. Students can see how their work compares to the standard. No part of asset-based teaching and learning is about lowering standards. Self-assessment is a way for students to see the standard and how their current level of work compares to it. Additionally, self-assessment can include multiple layers that allow students to see their strengths, even if they are not immediately recognized as academic strengths. Consider the following areas:

  - ▶ Holistic goal-setting with individual students: Focus on the strengths a student already has while looking forward to what the student would like to accomplish next. There is space for students to talk about what they would like to accomplish and consider how they may feel as they go through the process and arrive at the goal. Students can engage with the idea that they may have already accomplished hard things and that even though learning the new content may be challenging, they can lean on their life experiences to get through the social-emotional blocks to success.

  - ▶ Language objectives: All students are learning to use language more effectively, particularly students who are classified as language learners and would benefit by self-assessing their ongoing development of the four language domains (speaking, listening, reading, and writing).

  - ▶ Social-emotional learning objectives: School should be a place where we learn life skills like collaboration, goal-setting, and task orientation. Tracking these areas will allow students to practice with the particular language around these skills as they develop them.

  ▶ Social justice or cultural competency objectives: Again, allowing students to reflect on how their learning impacts justice is a critical idea. It allows students to wrestle with the content and their performance of the learning task in the larger arena of impacting the world around them.

- *Teacher assessment and feedback:* A fundamental practice of a good educator is assessing the learning and giving the students the feedback they need to continue their learning journey. Too often, teachers discuss assessment through the lens of what students still cannot do. There is such a strength, however, in framing the assessment as a celebration of what the student has demonstrated, with clear next steps to move that student forward toward progress.

  Ample amounts of educational research support the idea that feedback is one of the most powerful gifts a teacher can give students, especially when the teacher has taken the time to build students' beliefs that they can learn and grow. For example, a fifth-grade student who has completed a one-page paper and has demonstrated an excellent command of grammar and vocabulary may need further work on word choice. Teacher feedback that instructs the student to use a thesaurus to diversify word choice is a specific, actionable step to help the student improve their writing.

  We cannot emphasize enough how much of an impact teacher assessment and feedback can make, especially when rooted in an asset-based mindset. These practices help build positive relationships between students and teachers and the learning process itself. Students stop viewing grades as something given to them and better understand them, no matter how they are represented in their district, as calls to take the next step in the learning progression.

STEP 4: Adjust your instruction as student strengths change throughout the year.

The students who walk into a classroom at the beginning of a school year will be different students by the end of the year. Learning is a progression and not an endpoint. As our students progress and their strengths develop and shift, we can adjust the work we do with them.

We have recommended that you do everything you can to learn about your students' strengths at the beginning of the year, and it must continue throughout the school year. As students share new interests or develop new strengths, instruction for that student must change. An example of this is small-group work based on student levels. If a student's level increases, we must celebrate that progress. We must also acknowledge it by placing the student in an appropriate group.

OVERCOMING PUSHBACK

Nearly every teacher has had a student whose areas needing growth were so glaring that it was difficult to see the student's strengths. Those same teachers also probably know that when the student's strengths were highlighted, it made a world of difference. Don't worry about giving students a false sense of confidence. Think beyond the time it takes to offer specific feedback to each student. This Hack is well worth the time and energy. Here are a few common concerns about this Hack and how to address them.

Talking about a student's strengths gives them a false sense of achievement. A student's strengths are what they have achieved. Too often, we focus our conversation on the many things a student cannot do. However, we must turn our attention to what the student is already able to do, because that is the foundation on which we will build the next skills. Additionally, students need confidence in their abilities to take on new tasks. Talking about what students have already mastered allows them to view themselves as capable learners. It shows them that what was once a challenge is now an easily accessible skill.

What if a student has no strengths? Unfortunately, this is a real question teachers ask on occasion. We have heard this question regarding bilingual students who have not yet demonstrated a mastery of language, or students who, due to life circumstances, have not been in school and thus don't know any foundational skills for literacy or math. These situations can seem challenging for educators due to what appears to be an overwhelming discrepancy between those students and their peers. However, strengths exist. It may be that a student who is not yet reading has strong auditory receptive skills and comprehends complex instructions or stories if shared with them verbally. Students who are still learning the numerical symbols used to represent quantities may already have a great sense of problem-solving that lies in the skills necessary to live in a refugee camp. We must be willing to look beyond our traditional understanding of "academic strengths" and see those social, emotional, and life skills that are also strengths.

Offering feedback for every student is too time consuming. As is often said in education, we must slow down to speed up. Taking the time to offer feedback, including highlighting the strengths of a student's work, will pay dividends. It is the action of partnering with students to see what they have learned and what they can learn next. Again, the positive feedback offers a way for students to build confidence, and the areas for improvement give the student specific ways to move the learning forward. If this is not the purpose of education, then what is?

THE HACK IN ACTION

The following story is told by Lissette Jacobson.

I spent my years in the classroom working with students who were multilingual learners. It has not always come naturally to look at all students through the lens of their strengths, but I have developed this skill over time. The following story is an example of finding and amplifying the strengths of all students.

I always loved working with multilingual students and helping them discover their strengths, because I know the difference it would have made for me. As an eighth-grade ESL teacher, I was working with a group of students in preparation for a project that would result in the students giving a presentation. While public speaking is a common fear for many eighth-grade students, it is particularly challenging for students who are not confident in the target language. However, it aligned with the WIDA national language acquisition standards we used in Illinois and supported the speaking standards.

As I observed my students, I considered their diverse backgrounds and talents. There was Alejandro, a talented artist with a knack for visual storytelling, and Fatima, whose exceptional memory and organizational skills made her a natural researcher. Recognizing their unique strengths, I decided to incorporate them into the project.

Alejandro's artistic abilities came to life as he sketched beautiful visuals to accompany the group's presentation. His detailed drawings captivated the audience's attention. Fatima, with her exceptional memory, organized and structured the presentation's content, ensuring a smooth flow of information.

As the project progressed, I made a conscious effort to highlight each student's strengths. I praised Alejandro's creativity and Fatima's organizational skills, instilling confidence and motivation in them. The positive feedback served as a catalyst for the students, encouraging them to take ownership of their work.

The day of the presentation arrived, and the students took center stage with a newfound sense of confidence. Alejandro's visual aids complemented Fatima's eloquent delivery, creating an engaging and informative presentation. The audience was captivated by their hard work and ability to overcome linguistic barriers. I supported their linguistic needs by providing grade-specific and content-specific sentence stems to help them hit their speaking standards.

I believe this approach helped my students succeed in their project and fostered a positive and inclusive learning environment. By celebrating their strengths, I empowered my students to embrace their identities and cultures, transforming the classroom into a space where diversity was valued and celebrated.

Focusing on student assets instead of deficits is a research-based strategy for positively impacting student outcomes. All students have already accomplished skills and can achieve more. The following ideas will help you ACT on this Hack.

Actions:

- Take time to review your class roster and jot down the strengths of each student. If you come to a student for whom you cannot identify a strength, be intentional about spending time with that student in the following week to determine a strength.

- Work with students to help them self-identify their strengths. Then ask them to think about how they can build from those strengths and continue to improve as learners.

Consider:

- Review your general frame of reference for how you discuss students in your classroom or school. Do you usually frame conversations about struggling students around what they can or cannot do?

- Contemplate your current response to students in special programs in your school (such as special education, language learners, and reading intervention). Can team conversations include the strengths of these students and how the team can build on those strengths?

Turning Point:

- As more students enter American classrooms with home languages other than English, it is necessary to remember that the average multilingual student possesses a vocabulary much larger than monolingual students. We must leverage this linguistic repertoire.

- The belief that all students have strengths worth celebrating and investing in impacts the teacher's belief about students' future learning.

HACK
7

LISTEN TO UNDERSTAND
Decrease Disproportionate Discipline Patterns

*Too often we forget that discipline really means
to teach, not to punish. A disciple is a student,
not a recipient of behavioral consequences.*
— DR. DAN SIEGEL, PROFESSOR OF PSYCHIATRY

THE PROBLEM: CULTURAL COMMUNICATION BARRIERS LEAD TO NEEDLESS STUDENT DISCIPLINE

I N A MODERN school building, a plethora of issues get in the way of effective communication between students and teachers. It could be as recognizable as spoken language or as nuanced as body language. Still, situations occur in which the communication from a student or teacher is not understood by the other. In some situations, a simple clarification can correct it. In others, the issue escalates as the miscommunication is understood as disrespect. The disrespect then results in student discipline. As this is repeated, it eventually leads to exclusionary discipline.

Unfortunately, this situation does not fall evenly across the student body. We know that most teachers are White and female, and the average age is forty-two. However, our student body is growing more diverse. In the fall of 2021, 15 percent of students enrolled in public schools were Black, and 28 percent were Hispanic. These demographics indicate why there's an increased opportunity for intercultural mismatch. Schools tend to take on the majority culture. Since many of our schools are filled with middle-class White women, this culture and its accompanying norms tend to be elevated. Again, the way this plays out with our students of color has traditionally shown up in disproportionate discipline toward our Black and Hispanic students in particular.

When you add the mismatch between the youth culture and that of the older generations in the classroom, it leaves room for potential conflict. This conflict interrupts the teaching and learning process and is counterproductive to the feeling of community that we need in our classrooms. Issues can happen with any part of communication. It is important for teachers to understand what is said and how it is said. Tone, body language, and slang can cause a cultural mismatch and create moments of perceived disrespect. These perceptions of disrespect cause a divide in the classroom, and a classroom without rapport and alliance is a less effective, less culturally responsive classroom.

THE HACK: LISTEN TO UNDERSTAND

This Hack, in one sentence, is to listen to your students to hear what they are communicating, not what you are receiving. The concept of nonviolent, compassionate communication suggests that all behavior is a request. Students talk and act in certain ways as a method to get their needs met. At the root of this Hack is understanding that students, generally speaking, want to get their needs met. On top of that, we must understand that how they express their needs is deeply based in our culture, and people from different cultures may have differences in how they communicate. There is no one way to communicate. As those differences arise, they may appear in ways that are so different from another culture that they appear to be disrespectful, and this is where we need to take action. As educators, we must listen to the students in our spaces, and we must do so with an ear bent toward hearing them and working with them to meet their needs.

This Hack requires intentionality and some self-work, but it is worth it. If you implement this Hack with fidelity, it will decrease needless power struggles, increase the sense of empathetic connection, and increase the potential for learning by students of all cultural and linguistic backgrounds.

The act of listening across cultures is a complex task. It is a practice you must establish as a norm at the level over which you have control. It should be an expectation set for all participants in your classroom, and one that is talked about openly and directly. When a student does not make eye contact with you while conversing about the student's unexpected behavior, consider your own cultural norms, those of the student, and what is being communicated. If a young, Black, female student tells

TONE, BODY LANGUAGE, AND SLANG CAN CAUSE A CULTURAL MISMATCH AND CREATE MOMENTS OF PERCEIVED DISRESPECT.

you she's not *cappin'* while becoming visibly upset when a friend called her a liar, what cultural nuance do you have to understand in her impassioned response? From the elementary classroom to the secondary athletic field, communication across cultures is a key to ensuring that students from all backgrounds can succeed.

WHAT *YOU* CAN DO TOMORROW

In the realm of equity work, cross-cultural communication is one place where we can make progress. The following steps will help ensure that you are listening to your students to better serve them, and this requires some reflection, interrogating your definition of respect and the cultural values in which that definition is rooted.

- **Reflect on your concept of respect.** Ask yourself how you define respect. What does it look like? What does it sound like and feel like? Now ask yourself why you have that definition. You can best accomplish this activity through journaling or writing your ideas so you can think deeply about them. Once you have come to your conclusion, consider how you will make room for other lived experiences that produce other definitions of respectful communication in your classroom.

- **Reflect with your students and staff on the concept of respect that each person brings.** Unlike the prior activity, educators need to understand what expectations around respect others are bringing into the school. Ask students what respect looks like in their homes. Ask them how they interact with adults and other young people in their communities. Having a better understanding of the cultural norms that produce the behaviors your students exhibit will give you a stronger foundation to stand on when responding to that behavior.

- **Use a community-building circle to create class norms.** This process is rooted in restorative practices. If you are unfamiliar with this concept, you can find more information in *Hacking School Discipline* by Nathan Maynard and Brad Weinstein. The idea is that you work collaboratively with your students to create the norms for the classroom community. During this process, you ensure all students can share what they value in a community. Then, each student follows up with a statement about how to actionize that value. Encourage students to think about what is important to them as they interact in the community outside of school.

- **Practice listening.** Take time to teach listening and practice listening with your students. Here are a few intentional ways you can do this.

  ▸ *Draw the picture:* Give instructions and have students draw what you are describing. This allows students and teachers to interact in ways that build understanding.

  ▸ *A read-aloud:* This classic activity that fills the elementary school building is still a powerful tool at the secondary level. Reading a book aloud and engaging with students in interactive ways during the read-aloud asks students to practice their listening and comprehension skills.

  ▸ *Charades:* We may not realize that this classic party game is about listening, but it helps teachers and students remember that communication is more than verbal. Our body language says so much. This game can help clarify the differences in how we read one another's actions.

▸ *Scene work:* This activity is particularly great for students who are language learners. Show students a short scene from a movie or TV show, preferably one that is popular (and appropriate), and ask students to note what is being communicated. In the younger grades, it may be direct comprehension. In the older grades, it could also include insinuated ideas.

- **Trade "words of the day."** Youth culture is constantly producing new language and new ways to use current language. One idea to try to keep up while also promoting student agency and student voice is to participate in an exchange of "Word of the Day (or Week)" words. Ask students to bring in a word from their home language or a popular word in youth culture and share what it means and how it is used. In return, the teacher can present an academic word connected to the content or real life. This exchange will benefit both the students and the teachers.

- **When perceived disrespect is actually disrespect, ask why.** We need to make this statement: Sometimes, a student wants to communicate disrespect. The premise of this Hack is to decrease the likelihood that a cultural mismatch in communication styles will be perceived as disrespect. However, there are times when a student wants to communicate disrespect. In this case, we need to ask why. "Why is that student attempting to disrespect me, and how can I be a part of solving it?" When a situation gets bad, a student may be removed from the classroom, but that student may return to the classroom the next day. If there has not been an attempt to resolve the root of the student's conflict, it may still be there the next day. Asking why helps to get to the actual problem and begin resolving it.

A BLUEPRINT FOR FULL IMPLEMENTATION

Cross-cultural listening is a journey you must intentionally take while remembering that it is just that—a journey. You can repeat the steps in this blueprint to ensure you continue focusing on the task of listening.

STEP 1: Examine your values regarding communication.

Communication has many components, and each must be considered when examining our values about communication. Consider both the verbal and nonverbal components. Write these items down. List out the parts of communication and then describe how you practice each one. Ask yourself why you practice that part of communication in that way. For example, if an educator grew up in church where values were taught through Sunday school stories and expository preaching, the teacher may use storytelling as a teaching method. Also, we can learn to recognize the communication practices that do not sit well with us. Again, ask yourself why that communication style is problematic for you.

An example is when teachers struggle with overlapping talk, which is often rooted in a home experience or school experience in which the expectation was that one person talked at a time while all other participants listened. It's often partnered with the belief that if you are talking, then you are not listening and not learning. However, note that talking through new learning is a way to process information and see how it fits in with prior schema. This examination allows us to check our biases against certain forms of communication that may not be viewed as negative in another culture and may even be beneficial according to best practices.

THE GOAL IS FOR YOUR CLASSROOM TO BE A PLACE OF ONGOING CULTURAL LEARNING AND EXCHANGE.

STEP 2: Establish your classroom as a place for intercultural exchange.

The leader of a learning space sets the tone of the space. From the beginning of the year, set the tone that your classroom will be a place where everyone, students and staff, will learn from one another. In particular, ask students to bring their funds of knowledge into the learning space. Each student is already an expert on what and how they do things in their home and family. Some may even explain what concepts are important in their cultures as larger ideas.

For the sake of this Hack, further explain to your students that communication styles are an area in which you will exchange cultural norms. This step of establishing your classroom as a learning space for culture is key so that in the future, students can ask questions about culture in any direction without the fear of it being misconstrued as offensive. The goal is for your classroom to be a place of ongoing cultural learning and exchange.

STEP 3: Create classroom norms collaboratively.

Work with your students to create a collective understanding of expected classroom behaviors. A major part of the norms will be about how the learning community members communicate with each another. Step 2 established that all cultures would be welcome in the classroom, and the class can highlight this equity in the creation of norms. Ensure students bring their full selves to this conversation to create a classroom community that allows for different cultural expressions. Take the following actions:

1. *Explain the purpose of creating class norms.* Remind students that when you create norms together, it is like making a community pact. All students are a part of building the expectations together, all students agree to practice the norms, and all students can hold one another accountable to the common expectations.

2. *Ask students to share one value that is important to them in building a relationship.* Students, no matter their age, may need a list of words to choose from. The students might select words or phrases like trust, sense of humor, or honesty. Ideally, they would not repeat a word that has already been said unless that value is really important to them. The person leading the activity records the words or phrases to be visible to the class. When everyone is done sharing, check again to see if students want to add more words to the list.

3. *Guide students to turn one of the words or phrases into an affirmative command.* Give students the opportunity to take a word or phrase representing a value and turn it into an action statement. Generally, it should be affirmative, describing what they should do instead of what they should not do. An example might be that if the word is "honest," the command might be, "Always speak your truth." Or if the phrase was "equally engaged," the action could be "Be fully present" or "Participate to your fullest extent." Again, record these phrases in a visible spot. Remember that this activity works for all grade levels, even in the primary grades. You may need to adapt it to your students' vocabulary and scaffold it to their experiences.

4. *Narrow the list to no more than six to eight phrases.* Establish the norms as the go-to expectations for the classroom. Make them simple to read and understand, rather than a long list of items to remember. Once the list is written, work with the class to reduce the list, joining sentences or trimming sentences with similar or related messages. After you have narrowed the list, ask the students if anything is missing.

5. *Agree to the norms as a learning community.* As each student acknowledges agreement to the group-created norms, it sets the tone for how the classroom will move forward together. It is also a great reference point when unexpected behavior occurs. Remind students that they all agreed on these norms they helped to create. It increases the concept of accountability in students' minds.

STEP 4: Create a system for how to engage with conflict in the classroom.

Even with norms set up in the classroom, conflicts will occur. Whether a conflict began in the cafeteria, on the playground, or in the classroom, it can be destructive to the learning environment and result in unnecessary school discipline, especially if it is not dealt with. Students need to know the rules of engagement for conflicts and be ready to help resolve them, but for that to happen, a system must be in place, and it must have been taught and practiced. Create a system that applies to conflicts between students and between students and staff. All participants must be willing to engage in the process, which is worth noting because sometimes, the most challenging people involved in conflicts are the adults who are unwilling to step into the process for resolution. These precursors must be in place to have a well-designed system.

When designing a system for engaging in conflict, consider culture. In some cases, it's necessary to have a third party mediate between the two parties involved. However, the hope is that the two parties involved can operate without the guidance of another person and resolve the conflict themselves. One question a party should ask before beginning to work with the other party is where the root of the conflict is located. Is it rooted in cultural values? How might one person's expectations differ from another person's expectations? If the students are not at an age where they can do this thought exercise by themselves, a teacher can help them reflect. Once that question has been answered, it helps to set the table for creating a resolution grounded in not undoing anyone's cultural values.

Unfortunately, in many classrooms, the person whose values best align with the teacher or another leader gets to have their desired outcome. This scenario does not bring actual resolution and instead leaves the conflict to fester in the heart or mind of one party.

When we mention a system, we generally think of a conversation, often led by teachers. However, depending on the grade level you work with, you could devise a conflict resolution template and keep copies of it in your learning space. You could teach students to complete the form on their own and then come together to engage in a conversation to work toward a resolution. Setting up a system that can be led by a student or another adult is key so you can maintain your focus on instruction. It's worth the time on the front end because, even if you are focused on instruction, a student in conflict will not be focused on learning.

Finally, one piece of the system to intentionally teach and practice is the skill of listening to others. Whether listening only to respond or actively interrupting the other party, nothing derails conflict resolution more than the refusal to listen to one another. If students or staff are unwilling to listen, they may not be ready to participate in the conversation, and it may be necessary to take more time to listen. Notwithstanding, this is one reason that Steps 2 and 3 are so important. Those steps help to establish the room's culture as one of empathetic listening. In rooms where learning about one another's culture is the norm, students will already be used to listening and learning about new concepts and cultures. Those skills transfer over to resolving conflict. Listening across cultures is paramount.

OVERCOMING PUSHBACK

When it comes to addressing student behavior, a myriad of biases play a role. If we are to implement this Hack as a measure to reduce the disproportionality in exclusionary discipline toward students of color, students with special needs, or students from impoverished homes, it is necessary that we change the way we understand behavior. We can view it as a form of communication to be understood through a cultural lens. This type of change will be met with pushback, but the goal of the change is worth the effort. We will be able to resolve conflict, deal with disrespect, and teach personal accountability along the way.

Resolving conflict has nothing to do with my curriculum. It is a challenge to meet all the standards explicitly written into the curriculum of any content area. When you add the layer of making room for social-emotional learning in the form of conflict resolution, it certainly can feel overwhelming. Note that a brain in "fight or flight" mode is not a brain ready for learning. If students come into the classroom in conflict with the teacher or another student, their brains will not do their best learning. In this sense, resolving conflict is indeed a task that takes time. But it means slowing down in order to speed up, so it is key. An engaging classroom will be a place where students learn life lessons, not just lessons from a textbook. Taking the time to help students resolve conflict will create a powerful learning community, making students feel heard. This time and energy given to listening to students is an investment that will pay dividends in students' productivity and willingness to push for increased learning in the classroom.

Some of my students are just disrespectful. There are moments when a student is trying to communicate disrespect, in their culture and yours. In these moments, pause and ask why that student wants to be disrespectful. It comes back to the ability to communicate across cultures. It is perfectly okay to tell students that their behavior was perceived as disrespectful. Follow up by asking the students if being disrespectful was their intention and, if so, what they hoped to accomplish.

Again, while these situations of disrespect do arise, it is often the case that a motivating factor is at play. Even a novice teacher is aware that students bring their life challenges with them into the classroom. Students who are feeling lost or hopeless may lash out with disrespectful behavior. However, the root of this Hack is to ask oneself, "Is the behavior I am seeing actually disrespectful, or is it a perception rooted in my own cultural values?"

If all they do is talk it out, there is no accountability. Some educators, to reference the Shakespeare play *The Merchant of Venice*, want their pound of flesh when it comes to student discipline. They want to ensure that students are punished for their bad behavior. This pushback question emerges from this frame of thought. However, this Hack is based on the idea that the root word of discipline is "disciple or student." The idea is simple: School discipline is an opportunity to teach students ways to behave, handle their emotions, and communicate effectively across various settings. If a student has not yet learned the multiplication tables, we do not punish them. We practice with them, reviewing the skills and reteaching when necessary. We must take the same approach to school discipline.

Intentional listening across cultures is the definition of accountability. It requires a person who has potentially caused harm to someone else, intentionally or not, to engage in a conversation about how to better communicate. It asks both students and staff to be involved in the learning process as they learn about one another's cultural norms and perceptions of respect. If learning a lesson is the purpose of discipline, then a student sitting alone at a table during lunch recess will not accomplish the goal. Instead, ask them to practice the very skill they need to work on—communication—as a better approach.

THE HACK IN ACTION

The following vignette includes a conversation between a teacher (her name is a pseudonym) and author Maurice McDavid while he was in the role of a dean and a teacher.

It was a difficult conversation for Ms. Steward, a high school literature teacher. She was sitting with the dean of students, who was holding a stack of discipline referrals. The dean had been part of the team that had hired her, and he was confident in her teaching abilities. However, he was there that day to discuss a pattern he had noted in her referrals. The teacher had written referrals for eight students in the first quarter. All eight of the offending students were males, and seven were Black males. The one White male had received one referral, and three of the Black males had received multiple referrals. These were the facts of the situation.

The dean and Ms. Steward began the conversation by laying out the referrals on the table between the two of them. The dean started by stating that he wanted to ensure she knew she had the right to write referrals and that the deans wanted to support her in ensuring that her classroom culture was excellent. He then began to read off the names of the students with referrals and asked the teacher to call out what the students had in common. Aghast, the teacher blushed as she realized the commonality of the students. In that moment, she could choose to be offended or to do important work to correct what was happening in her classroom.

The correction began with a conversation about what the teacher thought was respectful behavior and what she viewed as disrespectful. The dean extended the conversation by asking, "Where do those values come from?" They went on to discuss that her understanding of what was and was not respectful was rooted in her values and that her students may have a different sense of what it means to be respectful. She agreed, and together they created a plan to learn more about the cultural backgrounds of all her students. Another part of that plan was that they would spend time practicing listening to one another. She was intentional about partnering with some of the students she had previously written up to try to hear what they were really communicating. Of course, even with these intentional efforts, conflict still arose in her classroom.

Ms. Steward returned to the dean's office and asked him to brainstorm the potential next steps with her. Together, they created a process specific to her classroom for dealing with conflict.

She designed her conflict resolution plan based on the literary ideas of conflict being part of a good story. She expressed that, without conflict, a story does not move forward. She also pointed out that conflict can be person versus person, person versus the world, or person versus oneself. She noted that, regardless of what type of conflict the students had in their stories, they could feel comfortable seeking a solution in her classroom.

Initially, the students were hesitant, but Ms. Steward continued to model it when conflict arose between her and a student. Then, one day, a small group of students working together on a project asked her to facilitate a resolution for their group. They resolved their conflict, and word of mouth spread quickly. Ms. Steward even began receiving visitors seeking help in resolving conflicts.

The rest of that school year, she only wrote four more referrals. She found that the system she had designed was effective, and she could better connect with all her students. In particular, she and her Black male students found ways to communicate more effectively. As they grew more comfortable with one another, they could stop and ask clarifying questions before jumping to conclusions.

Miscommunications due to tone and body language are common. However, adding the layer of cultural norms further complicates the essential task of understanding and being understood. Because communication is such a key part of the teaching and learning process, it is paramount that you take this new learning and ACT now.

Actions:

- Acknowledge that you communicate in a certain way and that it is not the only way. It is necessary to have this internal conversation with yourself and to be willing to have the other conversations mentioned in this Hack with others.

- Learn about the various ways communication takes place in your students' lives. One big topic you can study is the multiple methods of communication in youth culture.

Consider:

- A deep dive into your ways of communicating can be helpful for all interactions throughout the school day. What forms of communication do you consider to be respectful? How did you arrive at these norms?

- In many classrooms, students represent a variety of cultures, and it is challenging to be an expert on each one of them. How do you approach communication with families in general? Who will you talk with to learn all you can?

Turning Point:

- According to a 2018 report from the Aurora Institute, around 40 percent of students in American classrooms will identify as language learners by 2030. If, perchance, your classroom is not home to one of those students, you still face the task of working with students of a different generation. Youth culture has a drastic impact on language and communication. Learning a new way of communication will reduce misunderstandings and promote a class culture of trust.

- The world and the US are now places of such high mobility that it all but guarantees a teacher stepping into the classroom will teach a student whose home language is not English and whose home culture will not align with the school culture. With this in mind, now is the time to make a move to better communicate with students and avoid needless power struggles.

HACK
8

TREAT EACH LANGUAGE EQUALLY

Elevate the Status of Languages Other than Standard American English

All languages were bestowed with a garland of wisdom and possess knowledge, understanding and instruction to reflect the beauty of a particular culture. No language is superior or inferior.
— DAVID SSEMBAJJO, AUTHOR

THE PROBLEM: ELEVATING STANDARD AMERICAN ENGLISH LESSENS THE POSITIVE SENSE OF SELF FOR LINGUISTICALLY DIVERSE STUDENTS

AS OF 2019, around 23 percent of school-aged children in the United States spoke a language other than English at home, according to the Center for Immigration

Studies. This stat does not even consider the number of students who speak a vernacular of English at home, such as AAVE or Chicano English. Each distinct language, as well as each vernacular and dialect of English, is intimately connected with the identities of the students and families who speak it.

Students arrive at our schools having spoken the languages they have heard in their homes. Then they enter a building where Standard American English is taught. They hear words that end in "ing" where the "g" is present. They hear vocabulary words that have "false friends," having the appearance of a word in their home language but meaning something different. They will attempt to share themselves orally and may be reprimanded because their grammar does not match the English being taught. The students are corrected and told that their English is "improper."

Therein lies the problem. American education, for the longest time, has felt the need to tear down language that does not meet the state standards. And with the language, they have torn down the people who have received care and nurture in those derivations of English or in other languages. Language and identity are intensely connected; to disparage one is to disparage the other. When we describe the language students come into our classroom speaking as *ghetto*, improper, or uneducated, we are describing the mothers, cousins, and *tias* who speak that language in love. It is, by definition, a deficit-based mindset that is ineffective at producing a classroom culture of belonging and belief.

Instead, a refusal to acknowledge the language many students bring into the classroom as viable creates gaps in the reading outcomes for culturally and linguistically diverse students from kindergarten onward. Even in kindergarten, we treat students who do not speak Standard American English as if they need an intervention. The truth is that they have not yet received Tier 1 instruction that is effective for students learning a language. When teachers refuse to use students' skills or understand the language they speak and the rules that go with it, they ignore the strengths students already have. We could use those strengths to accelerate learning, but instead, we slow things down and create learning gaps for our students. This scenario does not reflect equitable education.

THE HACK: TREAT EACH LANGUAGE EQUALLY

When it comes to speaking more than one language, according to research published in November 2020 by the *Journal of Neurolinguistics*, over 50 percent of the world population is at least bilingual. Author François Grosjean, in his 2021 book *Life as a Bilingual*, estimates that up to half of the world speaks more than one language. In the United States, that number is less than half of the world average, around 21 percent.

While the number of students in our schools speaking a language other than English continues to grow, we draw attention to the additional students who speak another dialect of English. We call these students bi-dialectical. These linguistically diverse students bring an incredible amount of funds of knowledge with them into the classroom, but it is often missed because English, Standard American English in particular, is seemingly king.

EDUCATORS EMPOWER STUDENTS BY REMINDING THEM THAT AN ACCENT ON THEIR ENGLISH TELLS A STORY ABOUT THEIR FAMILY AND CULTURE.

We put forward that these other languages and dialects must be elevated in our classrooms across this country if we are to see more equitable instruction and learning for all students. We can take simple actions—from including visible text on the classroom walls in languages other than SAE to reading from authors whose texts were originally written in another language or dialect. Educators have many ways to elevate the status of diverse communication.

All educators set out with high expectations for their students. They desire to connect with them and believe they can succeed. This Hack is an incredibly beneficial tool for reaching all students. We do not believe that teachers intend to create a language hierarchy in their classrooms. However, especially if the teacher is monolingual, it is easy to do so. Imagine, however, how a student from an Urdu-speaking home may feel walking into a classroom and seeing a quote from Malala written first in Urdu and then translated into English. Educators empower students by reminding them that an accent on their English tells a story about their family and culture. Allow students to see that some of the most impactful words that have been said and actions that have been taken throughout history were not done in English. This realization helps students to see that while they need to learn SAE, it is not the only important language in the world.

Apart from the examples already given, you can find ample ways to elevate languages other than Standard English. It has long been noted that students who demonstrate strength in their first language are better able to learn a second language. One way to encourage this process is to ask students to tell a story in the language they would use at home. Then have them write the story in the same way they just told it. Next, have students analyze what they wrote. They can see what rules they used to form their sentences. The teacher, too, can see which rules the students used that match SAE and what explicit skills need to be taught.

Before moving on to reinforce the SAE rules, celebrate with the students their ability to communicate a story, and call out some of the incredible ways they accomplished that, even if it falls outside of SAE. This example shows how to find ways for students to use their languages to communicate key ideas. Ask students to describe key content vocabulary using their "home language." Have them make a metaphor or draw an infographic displaying their current understanding. All of these elevate the status of languages other than SAE. They intentionally use the students' current language as a building block to add more to their linguistic repertoire.

This Hack is applicable from the earliest grades through high school. We regularly share how our ability to communicate across multiple cultural settings has helped us be more effective educators and leaders. Students benefit from being able to hold on to their linguistic identity in so many ways. Using the language they already have can help students learn to read. Showing high school government students that power and politics do not only happen in English helps them view the world as a global society, not just an American one. Students feel more of a sense of welcome and belonging when they have a chance to see not only their images represented but also their languages.

WHAT *YOU* CAN DO TOMORROW

If you have made it this far, you know that communication is a key component of what we do as educators. We are constantly sending messages. Many of us, perhaps unbeknownst to us, communicate that English is the most important skill we can learn. However, in doing so, we fail to engage some of our students and thus fail to hit our goal of building English literacy. You can implement the following actions tomorrow to elevate the status of languages other than Standard English.

- **Consider the relationship between language and perceived IQ.** Over the last fifteen years, educators have had more and more conversations about bias. For example, when we hear someone with a British accent, we tend to think of that person as high-class or intelligent. When we hear someone with a US Southern accent, we tend to think of that person as less intelligent. The famous American comedian Jeff Foxworthy, who is from the South, said, "I used to say that whenever people heard my Southern accent, they always wanted to deduct 100 IQ points." As educators, we must be aware of how this shows up in our classrooms. If we are not aware, it can impact how we interact with students, staff, and families. Consider using the checklist on our website, blackbrownbilingue.com, to check for linguistic bias in your classroom.

- **Grow your knowledge about language and its production.** It's not hard to learn about languages and how new languages have been and are being produced. It is commonly known that William Shakespeare coined over a thousand words and phrases in his writing. For example, "All that glitters is not gold" comes from his play *The Merchant of Venice*. It's important to remember that language is still being invented today. Particularly within youth culture, we see new words and phrases and new meanings of existing words. Some people view this as the dissolution of "pure" language. However, in reviewing the history of language, we learn that language has always been fluid and evolving. Learning about the history of words and how they are formed allows you to be more open to the idea

that even Standard American English has evolved
to where it is today.

- **Talk with your students about global linguistic
  distribution.** Living in an English-speaking country
  makes it easy to think that the world speaks like
  you. However, your students may be surprised to
  know that only about one-seventh of the planet
  speaks English, and that many of them learned
  English as a second language. According to statistics by Babbel, nearly one billion people speak
  Mandarin Chinese as their first language. The
  second most common language as a first language is Spanish, with nearly half a billion people
  speaking it in their homes. Additionally, even
  though English is the most spoken language in the
  world, with 1.5 billion people speaking it, about 1.1
  billion of them learned it as a second language and
  probably have an accent. Students in your classroom with an accent can know they are not alone in
  the world.

- **Be intentional about using language to build community.** We are all language learners. A simple
  statement like this is a powerful way to affirm all
  students in the classroom: all students are learning
  a language, whether it is a first, second, or third
  language. Inside the classroom, you can use the
  multiple languages your students speak to build
  classroom routines, including greetings and simple
  instructions. It helps to create an inclusive environment. Acknowledge the multiple languages

students speak, and ask them to share new words and phrases used in their homes. Compare and contrast the languages spoken with English. Compare the English taught in the classroom with the dialects spoken in the classroom and around the world. All these small steps help to demonstrate the fluidity of language and help the students build a sense of community around the idea that they are all language learners.

- **Use social language to describe technical concepts.** While students may be learning Standard American English, they are experts in the language spoken at home. If students can communicate, then it should never be said that they don't have any language. Instead, educators must find a way to use the language they have as a building block. One way is to ask students to access their funds of knowledge and use what they already know to describe a new technical term. This request offers multiple areas of value.

  First, it requires the students to understand the new concept well enough to "translate" it. Second, it helps students connect the new learning with something they already know. We know that new learning must be added to the students' current schemas to move from short-term to long-term memory. Finally, this again promotes students' use of listening and speaking skills as they share their interpretations. Consider how students might describe a political party using terms from their social language. Some students might describe them as *two rival blocks beefin' over how to improve the community who sometimes lose focus on the community and end up fightin' over pride instead.*

- **Use ELL strategies for bi-dialectical students.** Often, when we think about language in our schools, it directly aligns with our English language learners. These students often speak a language other than English at home and have not demonstrated proficiency in academic English. Most states in the US offer ELL certification to show that teachers possesses the strategies necessary to support students learning English as an additional language. (We use this expression because some of our students already know two or three languages; thus, English is not a second language but an additional one.) However, we present the idea of using ELL strategies for bi-dialectical students because they come to us speaking a version of English that does not mesh with the English we teach. From the beginning of teaching reading, we see perceived deficits in our Black and Brown children. This discrepancy is rooted in the mismatch between their spoken English and the English taught for reading. One solution is to use ELL strategies for your ELL students and your bi-dialectical students. This requires intentional planning and implementation of these strategies based on the students' knowledge.

A BLUEPRINT FOR FULL IMPLEMENTATION

If you have grown up in the United States or have had American media as a major influence on your upbringing, it may seem that the English language rules the world. However, as our classrooms in the US and around the world continue to diversify, we must realize that language and identity are deeply tied together. As we find a way to amplify languages other than English, we also find a way to amplify our students. It will not happen by accident, though. The following thoughtful blueprint will get you moving down that pathway.

STEP 1: Co-create a language policy with students for inclusivity.

Involve students in developing a class language policy emphasizing respect for all languages and dialects to help set a clear, shared expectation that all forms of communication are valuable. For instance, during the first week of school, lead a discussion on language diversity and work with students to create a set of classroom norms, such as: "We respect all languages spoken here" or "We encourage sharing in any language."

Tune in to students' attitudes toward language. We have countless examples of children who grew up in an English-speaking home hearing Spanish spoken by a classmate and asking them to speak "regular." What do we consider "regular"? What value do we give to those who speak like us? How do we devalue those who do not speak like us? Taking time to reflect on our thoughts and feelings about language helps us be more thoughtful and purposeful when establishing how we will use language in the classroom and the school. All languages are created equal. All languages can facilitate the learning of another language.

STEP 2: Include language in your classroom procedures and community-building practices.

Whether or not you have multilingual learners in your classroom, you have ample opportunities to include languages other than SAE as you interact with students daily. Consider these ideas:

- Choose words from a language related to a topic you are studying or reading about in class. For example, if the class is studying the monarch butterfly's migration to Mexico, teach students the word for butterfly, fly, or migrate, and use it as a command to move from one place to another.

- Ask students to share a "Youth Word of the Day" to kick off class. Students can bring language from youth culture into the classroom and consider it on the same level as "academic" language. The students can then compare and contrast the word with a similar word from SAE.

- As students greet each other in the morning, teach the students greetings and how someone would respond in various languages. Those students in the classroom who speak a language other than English can take the lead and teach their peers greeting phrases.

STEP 3: Celebrate linguistic milestones.

Recognize and celebrate students' progress in learning new languages or dialects, whether they are improving in SAE, their home language, or an additional language. For example:

- Create a "Language Growth Chart" to track students' progress in different languages or dialects.

- Acknowledge multilingual achievements, such as students using a new word from another language or dialect in a project or discussion.

STEP 4: Include metacognitive linguistic analysis as part of the learning process.

At a most basic level, this Hack is an opportunity to remind all of our students that they are language learners. Metacognitive linguistic analysis is the idea of having students think about the language they are learning and using and, in particular, how they are learning it. When students think about their language acquisition, they can connect to the idea that other languages or dialects are also acquired. Because metacognition involves thinking about the learning processes by planning, monitoring, evaluating, and regulating them, it is an ideal time for students to pull from their full linguistic repertoire. During this think time, students can compare the new words they are learning to those they already know in any language. When learning science, students who speak a Latin-based or Greek-based language can apply their knowledge to learning suffixes, which helps them understand more new words. They can also highlight all the words in the English language that come from other languages. Here is a sample list of words and their languages of origin:

- alcohol – Arabic
- boss – Dutch
- pretzel – German
- resumé – French
- yogurt – Turkish
- zebra – Bantu

STEP 5: Expose students to multilingual media.

Include media (videos, music, podcasts) in various languages to expose students to the sounds, structures, and rhythms of different languages, fostering appreciation and curiosity. Teachers can use a short clip from a documentary or news source in another language, followed by a discussion about how language reflects culture. Another way to do this is to play songs in different languages as background music during independent work time and invite students to share songs they listen to at home.

STEP 6: Normalize code-meshing in oral and written communication.

Encourage students to blend their home languages or dialects with SAE in discussions and writing, reflecting real-world multilingual communication. One way is to provide assignments where students can use both their home language and SAE, and discuss how language mixing enriches communication. Additionally, encourage students to write creatively or academically in their home languages or dialects and provide space for sharing their work in multiple languages. Encourage students to write poems, narratives, or journal entries in their home languages, and display these works in the classroom alongside English versions. The nonverbal cues go far when elevating the status of other languages and dialects.

OVERCOMING PUSHBACK

The linguistic traditions of world cultures contain a richness. However, when so much of our educational system centers on English, it makes sense to hear pushback on this Hack. From feeling like your limited language skills keep you from accessing this Hack, to blind spots about "improper" English that may be present in you or those around you, we must push back on the pushback. Here are a few common concerns about this Hack and how to address them.

I don't speak another language, so I can't engage with other languages. This Hack does not require educators to know another language. It only requires that they be humble enough to learn something about another language and share that with their students. It's not about turning every classroom into a foreign language classroom but about bringing more languages forward in the classroom. We have traditionally disrespected languages other than Standard English. This Hack shows how to elevate those languages. In doing so, you elevate the status of the students who speak those languages and dialects, and you show students that the language they speak at home is valuable and honorable and can help them learn.

These dialects of English are improper English. English dialects such as African American Vernacular English and Chicano English are not "English with mistakes." These vernaculars generally have a set pattern that speakers follow and include ways of presenting ideas that SAE does not possess. For example, in Chicano English, the double negative follows the rules of Spanish. In Spanish, there is no rule against the double negative, so one might say, *"No quiero nada."* While we might translate this as "I do not want anything," the direct translation is "I do not want nothing." This example shows why students who use Chicano English would use the double negative as a consistent rule in their speech.

Consider another example from AAVE. The habitual "be" exists in AAVE and in many other languages but is hard to describe in SAE. The habitual "be" describes what a person usually or habitually is. It is often partnered with a verb in the gerund form. For example, Cookie Monster *be eating* cookies. Even if Cookie Monster is not eating cookies at the moment, he is the character from Sesame Street who *be eating* cookies. It is his habit to perform that action. This idea is part of why there are two forms of "be" in Spanish and even more in Japanese and Russian. AAVE is believed to be rooted in the English spoken by Scots-Irish immigrants working as indentured servants. The dialects spoken by that group included a habitual "be." This long-standing history demonstrates that language, in all its fluidity, is not proper or improper but depends on the context and purpose of the communication.

How will they ever perform on the reading tests if we allow them to speak this way? Students who come to our schools speaking a dialect of English other than SAE or speaking another language as their first language can still find success in school. It must be our absolute goal and commitment to ensure that success happens. However, our effort to see students excel on academic testing does not require that we denigrate the language our students speak at home, in the community, or in social circles. We do not need to restrict students' abilities to speak one language in order to instruct them to learn another. Students new to the country or who do not speak the language of instruction will often go through a silent stage, which may also be called pre-production. The student is taking in a new language but is not yet ready to produce thoughts in that new language. We must understand that this is

WE MUST ENSURE OUR STUDENTS KNOW THAT NO LANGUAGE IS BETTER THAN ANOTHER.

often the case for students who speak some form of English but are introduced to SAE. When given the opportunity to communicate in their known language or dialect, they can then engage in metalinguistic work to learn about the new language using the language they already know.

THE HACK IN ACTION

This story tells of the power of collaboration between two teachers (their names are pseudonyms) in a district where both authors worked. It represents the idea of esteeming each language as an equal.

Mr. Chasey, a fifth-grade dual language teacher, came to the library slightly frustrated. He was a Spanish language learner and loved the idea of being bilingual. However, he came to the library that day to brainstorm with Mrs. Totlam, the school librarian, to figure out how to increase his students' engagement with Spanish language books. Mrs. Totlam was familiar with the situation and knew that even though the school had twice as many dual language students as monolingual students (students receiving instruction only in English), English books were checked out at a rate of three or four to one in comparison to Spanish language texts. Mr. Chasey and Mrs. Totlam began brainstorming what they could do to change the culture in the classroom and the school.

After a while, they decided they needed to demonstrate to the students that Spanish and English were equally important and valuable languages. They had a few ideas about how to accomplish this. They invited Spanish-speaking school staff to read and review a book in Spanish. They recorded the staff reviewing the book in Spanish and shared the videos with students. Next, the teacher was intentional about reading books written in Spanish as they read texts aloud. Additionally, he chose books that centered youth culture and language. He asked the students to think about the languages they spoke, including *Spanglish*, a mix of English and Spanish, and compare it to the language in the books they were reading.

Finally, the teacher and librarian worked together to celebrate the lives of Spanish speakers in both the classroom and the library. The librarian collected biographies written in Spanish and others written in Spanish and English. This collection allowed students to practice reading in what seemed to be their language of preference. Inside the classroom, the teacher added bilingual posters featuring the people from the biographies and important quotes from them.

Through the intentional elevation of Spanish and Spanglish, the teacher increased the number of Spanish language books read in his classroom. The teacher and librarian felt strongly that their efforts were effective and could be replicated throughout the school building. They worked with the principal and the Building Leadership Team to create and implement a similar plan at the whole-school level. Bilingual posters filled the walls. The principal participated in the book reviews, sending one video per month, and other teachers followed suit. The librarian checked the data, and the results were clear. Students were checking out more and more Spanish or bilingual books. The librarian was excited when she noticed that even students from the monolingual classrooms were checking out bilingual books, wanting to read the same stories the teachers and principal were reading.

As educators, we bear the responsibility to model learning, respect, growth, and many other aspects of adulthood. In this way, some pundits are correct in that we hold an incredible influence over our students. As such, we must ensure our students know that no language is better than another. This belief is key for the sake of student academic performance and well-being. It's why we must ACT now.

Actions:

- Be intentional about the language you use to discuss language. Talk with your students about the richness of various languages in your classroom, community, and around the world so they will understand that the world does not run on English.

- Provide an opportunity for students to bring their language or dialect into the classroom. While you may not know another language or fully understand the dialect, you empower students and their languages by giving them time in the classroom.

Consider:

- Power and status are communicated directly and indirectly. What role does English play in your classroom? Does it hold all political power in your class or school?

- When we communicate about the worth of a language or dialect, we communicate about the worth of those who speak it. Do you believe that other languages are worth studying or discussing? In what ways can you promote this discussion? Where does it fit into your curriculum?

Turning Point:

- While the United States of America has no official language, most, if not all, governmental work is completed in English. This creates a level of importance assigned to Standard American English. While English is, indeed, an important language, it is necessary to elevate the status of all languages, including English with an accent and various dialects of English, as they are part of the identity of the students we teach.

HACK
9

TELL THEM WHAT THAT WORD MEANS
Build Vocabulary Through Meaningful Practice

The more words you know, the more clearly and powerfully you will think ... and the more ideas you will invite into your mind.
— WILFRED FUNK, AUTHOR AND PUBLISHER

THE PROBLEM: VOCABULARY DIFFERS AMONG STUDENT GROUPS

READING IS FUNDAMENTAL to student success, and it is made up of the ability to decode written language and make meaning of the words. The latter part of the definition is where vocabulary is key. Some students have broken the code of reading and can decode words but still struggle academically because their challenge is in comprehension. They come across unfamiliar words in their reading and lose meaning due to the missing vocabulary.

Beyond the skill of basic reading comprehension, some students face the additional challenge of academic- and content-specific vocabulary. Many students struggle to perform on assessments or in certain content areas because a vocabulary gap exists. When students do not understand what a question is asking, it is nearly impossible for them to appropriately respond. In some cases, students are not missing the content or skill they are being asked to share or demonstrate but are unable to perform the academic tasks because they lack clarity about what is being asked.

Unfortunately, there is a statistical pattern in the students with lower vocabularies. Even as early as pre-K, children from impoverished homes display fewer words in their vocabulary. Of course, if a student is growing up in a home where the family speaks a language other than English, the student enters school with a lower English vocabulary. They generally have an increased vocabulary overall since they know vocabulary in more than one language. Vocabulary is one factor in disparate reading data among various student groups, and it's a major problem for schools that are supposed to be producing equitable opportunities and outcomes.

To add to this problem, the response to this vocabulary gap has often been to teach vocabulary in isolation. Teachers have introduced new vocabulary through "drill and kill" using rote memorization. They introduce it at the beginning of units but then avoid using the language throughout the unit for fear of the words being too challenging for struggling students. They lower their vocabulary level to ensure students comprehend their instruction, but they have not asked the students to rise to the challenge of acquiring new vocabulary. This experience has left many students unable to access higher-level texts and unprepared for high-level assessments.

THE HACK: TELL THEM WHAT THAT WORD MEANS

This Hack applies what we already know about the language acquisition that takes place at a young age. Children learn language through interacting with it. That is, they hear language and are expected to produce language in response. The National Institute of Health says that children who only hear language on a TV or radio are far less likely to develop language. Young children develop language when they are spoken to in ways that invite them to speak back to the person. We can apply this same idea to the ongoing development of language and, in particular, the building of vocabulary.

It is not sufficient to simply present language to students without expecting them to use it. It's like the child who sits next to the radio or in front of the TV and hears the language but does not have the load of producing language. When, instead, there is an expectation of conversation between the person already possessing the vocabulary and the student learning it, the student is better able to process the word's meaning. Importantly, the words must be within the students' zones of proximal development so they do not shut down in response but instead take on the words as a challenge.

The action of this Hack is to provide students with opportunities to develop a deep, connected understanding of a word and then practice using it. To develop a high level of understanding of the word, students must do more than be familiar with its dictionary definition. Help students learn synonyms and antonyms of the word while also understanding what part of speech it is and how to use it in other parts of speech. The pupils benefit from seeing the word used in the real world, such as in news articles or on a website. An additional idea is to connect the word to concepts students already know. In doing this, they find ways to connect the word to their current schema.

After all of that, students still need to use the word. Create opportunities for them to use the word in their conversations and writing. Initially, you may need to provide a sentence stem that includes the vocabulary words, but in time, the students will add it as they engage with the content. Ask them to identify new words they need to add to their vocabulary to increase the meaningfulness of the words.

Undoubtedly, vocabulary lessons are highly effective when they are deeply rooted in creating meaningful experiences for students. These experiences allow them to actively contribute and engage within the learning community, enriching the overall learning environment. This idea of teaching vocabulary as part of a meaningful lesson is not new or radical but is incredibly impactful. Having a limited vocabulary holds students back from accessing new learning. Students with an increased vocabulary and the skills necessary to learn new vocabulary have an open door to ongoing learning. What is interesting about vocabulary acquisition is that it is necessary for both college and career readiness. Every field requires workers to learn job-specific terms. As students learn more words, it becomes easier for them to learn the next words.

Whether in a science or math class at the high school level or during language arts in a second-grade dual language classroom, teaching vocabulary in context is key. In those content-heavy classrooms, the vocabulary helps students access the high-level concepts and talk about details like an industry expert. When students are still developing the foundational reading skills, vocabulary gives them a well from which they can draw while they are decoding. Students familiar with a word and its meaning will decode it more easily, knowing that the word makes sense in the context of what they are reading. Across the board, teaching vocabulary in meaningful ways will support the overall growth of all our students, especially those with the greatest academic needs.

WHAT *YOU* CAN DO TOMORROW

Whether a school district has a predetermined vocabulary curriculum or each classroom creates its own, you can improve your vocabulary instruction tomorrow. The following items will produce high levels of understanding of both reading and content.

- **Frontload vocabulary and review throughout a unit.** At the beginning of a unit of study, select a limited number of vocabulary words that the students need to know to be successful in this unit. Pre-teach these words with the class, asking the students to create an ongoing list of words. Consider using the vocabulary templates shown in Table 9.1 and Table 9.2. Be sure to build in times throughout the unit for students to pull out the sheet to reference the vocabulary list they created at the beginning of the unit.

Word:

Morphology
(other forms of the word):

-

Part of Speech:
Noun Verb Adjective Adverb

-

In My Words (connotation):

-

-

Dictionary (denotation):

Example (sentence):

Table 9.1: Vocabulary template

English Word:	Cognates/Related Words
Spanish Word:	(either language):
Part of Speech:	•
Noun Verb Adjective Adverb	
	•
Definition in English:	
	•
	•
Definition in Spanish:	
Example Sentence (either language):	

Table 9.2: Vocabulary template for English language learners

- **Build in opportunities to apply vocabulary.** Find intentional and authentic ways for students to use the vocabulary that has been instructed. You can do this through writing or in conversation. Include the vocabulary in a question you ask students, and have them answer the question by using the question in their answer. Lead the students in an open-ended discussion that requires them to use the vocabulary in the form in which they learned the word but also challenges them to use the word in other forms. An easy way to engage students in applying the vocabulary is through a meta-cognitive analysis of the words. Ask students to discuss the vocabulary and their interaction with the words. Have they read it or used it before? In what contexts have they seen the word? In what settings are they likely to see the word or use the word again?

- **Use visuals and movement to teach and practice vocabulary.** Total physical response (TPR) is a highly recommended strategy for teaching vocabulary to multilingual learners. However, like many ESL strategies, it can be just as effective for other student groups. TPR is a method of teaching that uses physical movements connected to the meaning of a word to teach vocabulary. An additional step you can take is to ask students to come up with their own motions as they become more familiar with the word. They can also process learning a new word by illustrating the meaning. Whether it is content-specific or academic vocabulary, students must grapple with the meaning of the word to represent it visually. This representation does not have to be a drawing; it could be a digital creation that represents the meaning. Having students deal with the word in multiple areas of the brain helps to secure the learning.

A BLUEPRINT FOR FULL IMPLEMENTATION

If you teach young readers to read, you know that the simple view of reading can be broken into word recognition and language comprehension. That is to say that students must be able to decode words, but we also know they must be able to understand the words. Both decoding and understanding can be taught through intentional vocabulary practice, and it's why we have taken time to share a designed approach to vocabulary in your classroom. The following steps will help you implement this approach.

STEP 1: Identify tiered vocabulary (common, academic, and content).

Vocabulary tiering can look different depending on the level and topic of the classroom. The three main types of vocabulary are common, academic, and content. Common vocabulary includes words used in everyday language, such as "dog" and "house." Academic vocabulary includes words used in school and academic settings, such as "hypothesis" and "synthesis." Content vocabulary includes words specific to a particular subject area, such as "atom" and "molecule" in science.

While preparing for a unit of instruction or a lesson, it's wise for an instructor to consider what words the students need to know and understand to best interact with the learning for the day. The words may include vocabulary from all three tiers. A quick reminder that while not all teachers are reading teachers, all teachers teach reading. With this in mind, common vocabulary may still be significant in content classrooms like math, science, and social studies. Once you have identified the key words, consider how to teach them initially and then how to review them throughout the unit. In the review process, include opportunities for students to use the vocabulary in application. That, again, could be through writing a lab report, describing the steps necessary to solve a binomial equation, or conversing with a shoulder partner.

STEP 2: Integrate language standards into the unit of study.

One way you can intentionally build vocabulary practice into your classroom is by implementing language standards. In some states, the WIDA standards are used to support students identified as ELL. These standards ask students to practice English in all four domains of language: reading, writing, speaking, and listening. In states currently using Common Core State Standards, specific standards are connected to reading and writing. However, there are also standards connected to speaking and listening and vocabulary acquisition. Consider these standards when designing units of study.

A QUICK REMINDER THAT WHILE NOT ALL TEACHERS ARE READING TEACHERS, ALL TEACHERS TEACH READING.

Remember that it is possible to hit more than one standard at a time, and it is likely impossible to hit all standards for a grade level if you do not hit more than one at a time. Consider language usage and vocabulary acquisition standards when setting goals for student learning. While the main goal of a math lesson may very well be that students can add and subtract digit numbers across zeros, it is more accessible when students are required to know, understand, and use the word digit within a mathematical context. By using the language standards, students will be reminded that linguistic input and output are necessary to demonstrate their learning. As we help to develop our students' language, we give them greater access to the next learning levels.

STEP 3: Design learning experiences that allow for application of the vocabulary.

Once you have taken the time to tier the new vocabulary to your students, and you have layered in language standards to help set the direction of vocabulary learning, it is necessary to design activities for students to meaningfully engage in practice with the vocabulary. Students often get the chance to become familiar with a new language by reading and hearing it but do not always get the opportunity to add the vocabulary to their linguistic repertoire. This procuring of new vocabulary is best done by using the word in various ways. Here are a few activities you can use:

- **Analyze multiple-meaning words.** Have students create a chart that includes the multiple meanings of a word. They could list the phrases that include the word and then consider the similarities and differences. (For example, "running the race" versus "the car is running.") They could also describe how the word's meaning might change depending on the content being studied. (For example, "product" in economics versus mathematics.)

- **Connect to old vocabulary.** As students learn new vocabulary, have them create a "web of connected words." Students can think about what words they already know that are similar to the new word to help them cement the new word into their long-term memory by connecting it to their current schema. (For example, "Mitosis is like the words reproduction and divide, and it has to do with DNA.") This practice might also include connecting the new vocabulary to words that have meaning in the students' communities but are not part of Standard American English.

- **Describe a larger process that requires specific vocabulary.** Ask students to describe a multistep process that requires them to differentiate between steps using the new vocabulary. Offer predetermined scenarios from industries connected to the content, or ask students to create the scenarios. Be sure to include the expectation that vocabulary is specific. We measure what matters. Students should know that vocabulary matters.

- **Give students practice assessment questions that include the academic vocabulary they will see on assessments.** State assessments should not be the first time students see words like analyze, summarize, and interpret. As educators, we often take the language from a state standard and put it in student-friendly language. However, in doing so, we are sometimes not being friendly toward our students, who then must take assessments that include words from the standards they have not seen. Instead, we can provide students with opportunities to interact with academic vocabulary words. Try using practice questions, which you can find on many test websites or create with artificial intelligence apps.

OVERCOMING PUSHBACK

Educators often wonder which words they should teach. They also want to know how kids will respond to content-specific and other academic words. They worry that they are teaching to the test. However, vocabulary acquisition and the associated skills are pertinent to the future work students will do. Here are a few common concerns about this Hack and how to address them.

Vocabulary is just a spelling list or teaching to the test. Some teachers think about and teach vocabulary in isolation from the content. When done in this manner, yes, vocabulary can be a spelling list or test prep. However, when planning lessons that intentionally integrate vocabulary acquisition and usage, it is much more transformative. It becomes part of the learning itself. Vocabulary instruction is central to the lesson objectives. After all, students must be able to ask and answer questions about the content. They must be able to read and write about it. They should be able to do so at a high level, and we know that high levels of academic conversation include academic and content-specific vocabulary.

The kids won't understand what I am saying. This is why we must teach vocabulary and emphasize the words used in assessments and specific content areas. Everyone benefits when we maintain high expectations. In many cases, students do not know what we are teaching them until we teach them. Imagine someone saying we should not teach addition because students don't know how to add. We understand that students may struggle to understand addition until they understand the idea of quantity. In the same way, using content-specific vocabulary and academic vocabulary requires teaching all content with a greater depth. All students need this, especially those coming from historically underserved groups.

We have too many words to teach. There is no way around this truth. The English language has more than 150,000 words (currently in use) and even more definitions, with some words having multiple meanings. With this in mind, it certainly is a challenge to narrow down the list of words to teach in each grade level. Considering that students may have four to six different subjects they are studying throughout the day, it can be overwhelming. However, it is incredibly valuable to teach not only the vocabulary words as they are but also other forms of the words. For example, in a science classroom, students will likely learn the word "hypothesis." They should also learn the verb form, which is "hypothesize." Students might also learn how the prefix *hypo* and suffix *thesis* help to define this word. That gives them the additional knowledge necessary to independently learn other words that include these word parts as they progress through school. The skill of learning new words, whether through context clues or the direct instruction of word parts, is key to vocabulary instruction.

If a student is already behind in reading, we don't have time to teach vocabulary. Quite the contrary is true. Teaching vocabulary explicitly, especially as it becomes more specialized and complex, will improve students' comprehension. The explicit teaching of vocabulary will allow students to come to a new word and, even if they struggle to decode it, have an understanding of its meaning and thus improve their understanding of the text. There is still the question of time. Teaching vocabulary does not have to be complicated. We can integrate it into the beginning of the unit and then, as mentioned earlier in this chapter, include its explicit use and review in the remainder of the unit.

THE HACK IN ACTION

The following anecdote is based on Lissette Jacobson's experience with a middle school student she mentored, Luz (her name is a pseudonym).

Luz was a great student. She worked hard and was intent on attending college, where she wanted to study science as she prepared for medical school. Luz's science teacher felt like she was a strong student but noticed that vocabulary was challenging for her. Her teacher wrote it off to Luz being a language learner who was only a year and a half out from being classified as a newcomer. Luz and her family had arrived in the United States from Colombia about two years prior.

In her junior year of high school, Luz excelled in many of her classes and picked up quite a bit of social English. In her junior year, she challenged herself and enrolled in biology. They were in the middle of their unit on the human body, and Luz was struggling to remember some of the many challenging vocabulary terms. As they discussed the respiratory system, the teacher asked the class if they knew the major organs in the pulmonary system. The teacher, who was also bilingual, looked at Luz. Luz initially froze. The teacher wrote the words "pulmonary system" on the board and underlined the letters "pulmon." At that moment, something clicked for Luz, who knew that the Spanish word for lungs was *pulmones*. Luz answered confidently, "The lungs!"

The teacher went on to explain that in biology, many of the

words had Latin roots, and those roots were shared with many words in Spanish and Portuguese. In doing this, the teacher gave students an additional lens for learning the vocabulary. Not only were there many students who spoke Spanish as a first language, but many students had taken Spanish as an elective in high school. The teacher ensured the students were using the content-specific language in the remainder of the unit. For example, students had to research potential medical problems that can happen with the pulmonary system. They presented on topics like pulmonary embolisms (blood clots in the lungs) and COPD (chronic obstructive pulmonary disease). The students left the unit with a clear understanding of what the term "pulmonary" meant.

Across the nation, schools are realizing that students have struggled to learn foundational literacy skills like phonics, phonemic awareness, and initial letter sounds. As a response, schools have begun to focus their instruction in these areas in elementary school and as an intervention in late elementary and beyond. However, as discussed in this Hack, an additional key component to building strong readers is the purposeful development of vocabulary. Educators must ACT if we are to help raise literacy rates.

Actions:

- Make vocabulary a part of everything you teach. Whether it is a lesson in SEL, math, or physical education, find opportunities for students to learn new words.

These words may be content-specific or simply words they need to know for accessing education in general.

- Change how you plan your lessons. As much as you may want to include vocabulary, it will not happen by accident. Add a place in your lesson planning document or notebook to write the words you will teach this week.

Consider:

- The number of words students may encounter throughout their academic careers is so high that there is no way you could teach them all. How can you support students in taking on new words? What strategies do you have in your toolbox to help students learn new words on their own?

- Students may know a word's meaning but not in the target language. How do you assess a student's full linguistic repertoire? Are you aware of the cognates between the student's language and the target language?

Turning Point:

- Vocabulary is a primary pathway for students to build background knowledge, giving them access to more complex texts as they progress through the education system. Additionally, vocabulary helps students develop deeper connections. As we face reading challenges across our nation, taking on the challenge of growing students' vocabulary will give you a high return on investment.

HACK
10

THINK LANGUAGE!
Plan with Language in Mind

The limits of my language mean the limits of my world.
— LUDWIG WITTGENSTEIN, PHILOSOPHER

THE PROBLEM: TEACHERS FEEL RELUCTANT TO EMBRACE TEACHING LANGUAGE

EDUCATORS OFTEN VIEW themselves as specialists in certain subjects or grade levels. It is a common misconception that language learning only occurs in language classrooms. In reality, language is an integral part of all content areas and is crucial in how students acquire knowledge. While subject-level expertise is necessary for delivering quality education, all teachers should possess linguistic competence, which means the ability to effectively communicate and use language in a way that promotes learning. Teachers who view themselves as language teachers can significantly impact education and student learning.

The impact of not recognizing oneself as a language teacher can manifest in students struggling to comprehend and learn new concepts, partly due to poor communication from their teachers. When teachers are not equipped with strong linguistic skills, they may have difficulty explaining ideas clearly or answering questions effectively. This lack of linguistic skills can create a barrier between the teacher and student, hindering the learning process. Furthermore, when teachers do not prioritize linguistic competence, they may use language that is too complex or technical for students to understand, leading to confusion. Whether explaining complex mathematical concepts or discussing historical events, effective teachers rely on language. Yet, many teachers do not see this connection and may feel intimidated by the responsibility of teaching language in addition to their subject areas.

THE HACK: THINK LANGUAGE!

We all know the importance of planning and preparing for our lessons. We carefully consider the learning objectives, materials, and activities to ensure our students receive a meaningful and engaging learning experience. However, the crucial aspect of language is often overlooked.

WE CAN CREATE AN INCLUSIVE CLASSROOM ENVIRONMENT THAT SUPPORTS ALL LANGUAGES AND CULTURES.

Embracing language-focused instruction is not just a theoretical concept; it's backed by extensive research. Countless studies have indicated that multilingual students who received integrated language and content instruction perform better academically than those who received separate language instruction. Furthermore, a 2015 National Institutes of Health study found that classrooms that fostered a multilingual environment saw increased student engagement and decreased disruptive behaviors. Finally, Jim Cummins's 1981 research still has applications and value for educators today. In his paper titled "The Role of Primary Language Development in Promoting Educational Success for Language Minority Students," he suggested that proficiency in a student's native language contributes positively to developing proficiency in a second language, thereby enhancing overall academic achievement.

In light of these findings, it becomes indisputable that a language-focused approach to instruction can lead to more effective teaching and learning. To make it work in different environments, teachers can collaborate with their colleagues to share resources and strategies. Additionally, schools can provide professional development opportunities for teachers to learn more about effectively incorporating language into their lesson planning.

When we plan instruction with language in mind, we are taking a proactive approach to address the needs of multilingual students. We can create an inclusive classroom environment that supports all languages and cultures. Some solutions to incorporate language into lesson planning include:

- **Dual language books:** Utilizing dual language books in the classroom allows students to read the text in English and their native language side by side, which expands students' vocabulary, enhances reading comprehension, and provides an opportunity for students to share and connect with their cultural backgrounds.

- **Multilingual word walls:** Incorporating multilingual word walls in the classroom can be a valuable visual aid for students. The walls can display key vocabulary words in English and other languages spoken by students in the class. This display aids in vocabulary development and promotes a sense of inclusivity.

- **Language comparison activities:** Teachers can design activities where students compare grammatical structures or vocabulary across languages. For example, an activity might involve comparing how past-tense verbs are formed in English and Spanish. This comparison deepens students' understanding of both languages and facilitates a cross-linguistic transfer of skills.

- **Culturally responsive texts and materials:** Teachers can use texts and materials that reflect the cultures and experiences of their students. For instance, a social studies lesson about holidays could incorporate discussions about cultural celebrations around the world. This approach enhances content understanding, validates students' cultural identities, and promotes respect for diversity.

- **Collaborating with language specialists or bilingual teachers:** Excellent educators are always learning. Take full advantage of colleagues in your school who have their ESL endorsement or are experts in language acquisition. As you learn from your peers with expertise in this area, keep in mind that, as we mentioned in Hack 2, many of these strategies will benefit your students who come to school speaking a variety of vernaculars or dialects.

The benefits of planning instruction with language in mind are numerous. For one, it creates a more inclusive and welcoming learning environment for all students. Those from diverse linguistic backgrounds will feel valued and represented in the classroom, improving their sense of belonging and motivation to learn. Also, incorporating language into lesson planning can lead to better academic outcomes for monolingual and multilingual students alike. By acknowledging and supporting languages, we provide students with opportunities to develop their language skills further while enhancing their understanding of content areas.

Incorporating language into lesson planning may seem daunting at first, but you can seamlessly integrate it into daily teaching practices. For example, during class discussions, allow students to share their thoughts and ideas in their native languages to foster a more meaningful and authentic learning experience. Teachers can also incorporate cross-linguistic activities where students compare and contrast vocabulary or grammar rules between languages. This practice supports multilingual students' understanding of English and allows monolingual students to gain exposure to other languages and cultures. Additionally, incorporating culturally responsive teaching practices, such as using proverbs or idiomatic expressions from diverse cultures, can make the content more relatable and engaging for all students.

In any educational environment, versatile strategies can help create effective instructional planning with a language focus. In a physical classroom setup, teachers can create a "language-rich" environment with multilingual displays, posters, and materials around the classroom. Collaboration among teachers who teach different subjects can help integrate a language focus in diverse lessons, making language learning a schoolwide effort.

In virtual classrooms, digital tools and platforms can increase the inclusion of diverse languages. For instance, translation tools can help students comprehend information in their native languages, and discussion forums can encourage them to share their thoughts in their preferred languages. For homeschooling or one-on-one tutoring environments, teachers or tutors can personalize their approach using materials and resources in the learners' native languages and making real-world connections to the content.

Finally, in multicultural classrooms or environments with a high degree of linguistic diversity, teachers can encourage peer learning, where students teach each other words or phrases from their languages, fostering language development and cultural exchange. Thus, you can plan instruction with language in mind and effectively implement it across various educational settings, promoting inclusivity and improving learning outcomes.

WHAT *YOU* CAN DO TOMORROW

This section explores practical ideas and strategies teachers can use tomorrow to plan their lessons with language in mind. These activities, actions, and ideas are based on the four language domains—speaking, listening, reading, and writing—and aim to promote intentional oracy and model academic language. By incorporating these strategies into their teaching, educators can create a language-rich environment that supports the academic development of all students. Let's look at how you can implement these ideas in your classroom.

- **Review your teaching standards for the four language domains: speaking, listening, reading, and writing.** By understanding what is expected from students in terms of language, educators can plan their lessons accordingly and provide targeted instruction. This planning will help students meet academic expectations and foster language development. Teachers can use these standards to guide lesson planning and ensure all students have equal opportunities to practice and improve their language skills.

It's crucial to understand and incorporate students' language proficiency levels when planning lessons around the teaching standards. Proficiency levels can range from beginner to advanced, and as a teacher, it's essential to tailor your approach to correspond with these varied levels. Beginners may need more support with vocabulary and basic sentence structure, while advanced learners might be more ready to engage in complex text comprehension and academic writing.

- **Consider using formative assessments to gauge language proficiency.** These types of assessments provide vital feedback you can use to modify subsequent teaching and learning activities. After evaluating your students' language proficiency, align your teaching strategies and activities to meet their needs. This work could involve adapting materials to simplify language for beginners or providing more challenging texts to advanced learners.

  Moreover, incorporating language proficiency into your teaching standards doesn't mean teaching language in isolation. Instead, it's about integrating language learning into every subject and making it part of the content instruction. This way, students aren't just learning language; they're using language as a tool for learning.

- **Incorporate intentional oracy.** Another practical idea for teachers to implement tomorrow is to promote intentional oracy in the classroom. Oracy, in an educational context, refers to the development and enhancement of students' abilities to express themselves effectively and comprehend spoken language. It encompasses a broad range of skills, including vocabulary usage, articulation, fluency, and the ability to understand, formulate, and present a coherent argument.

  In schools, oracy is about providing students with opportunities to practice and improve these skills in a supportive and structured environment. It is equally about teaching students to be active listeners who can absorb, interpret, and respond thoughtfully to spoken information. The goal of fostering oracy in schools is to empower students to become confident communicators who can interact effectively in various situations and contribute to discussions in meaningful ways. This work involves creating a safe and supportive environment where students can communicate effectively and confidently.

  Teachers can encourage students to participate in discussions, debates, presentations, and other speaking activities that promote critical thinking and develop language skills. By providing opportunities for intentional oracy, educators can help students become active listeners, articulate speakers, and critical thinkers.

- **Model academic language.** Several strategies can help you effectively model academic language in the classroom, including:

  ▸ *Think-alouds:* Use the think-aloud strategy to make your thinking processes explicit to students. For example, verbalize your thoughts while solving a complex mathematical problem to demonstrate how academic language is used in problem-solving.

  ▸ *Sentence stems:* Provide sentence starters or frames to scaffold students' responses in academic language. During a discussion on a history topic, you could provide a stem, such as, "An important cause of the event was ..."

  ▸ *Explicit vocabulary instruction:* Introduce new vocabulary in context and provide opportunities for students to use the words in their speaking and writing.

  ▸ *Class discussions:* Engage students in classroom discussions on various topics. Model how to use academic language during these discussions and provide constructive feedback on students' language use.

  ▸ *Modeling through writing:* Demonstrate the use of academic language through written samples. By presenting students with examples of good academic writing, you can illustrate how to incorporate academic language into their work.

Remember, modeling academic language is not a one-off activity but an integral part of everyday instruction. Additionally, educators must understand the difference between home language and academic language. While students communicate and express personal experiences with their home languages, they use academic language to play a crucial role in their success. It allows them to access, engage with, and express complex ideas and concepts. As educators, we must recognize and value both types of language, bridging the gap between the two to promote a deeper understanding and mastery of academic language among students.

A BLUEPRINT FOR FULL IMPLEMENTATION

Twenty-first-century educators are used to using standards to drive their lesson design and implementation. Rarely, however, are those standards specific to language. For students labeled as language learners and those who have nearly mastered a language, we must think about how we are asking students to use language in both the front end and back end of teaching and learning. Follow these steps as a guide.

STEP 1: Inventory the linguistic diversity in your class, along with students' language needs.

This first step requires foresight to understand the linguistic makeup of your class. This understanding includes identifying the diverse languages your students speak and understanding their individual language needs. By taking the time to inventory this linguistic diversity, you can better tailor your teaching approach and materials to meet the needs of all students.

To begin, list all the languages your students speak. You can ask them directly or have them fill out an "about me" poster to help you get to know your students. Once you have identified the languages, research each language's unique features and challenges. This learning will give you a better understanding of where your students may struggle with certain concepts or skills due to their first language influence. This step may require seeking assistance from colleagues or experts in specific languages.

STEP 2: Find resources to build capacity (materials and people).

After taking inventory of the linguistic diversity in your class, find resources to help build your capacity as a teacher. These resources can include materials such as textbooks, workbooks, online resources, and other teaching aids. They can also include people such as colleagues, mentors, teacher trainers, or specialists in languages or language teaching methodologies. Access to these resources can help you improve your teaching skills and better meet the needs of your diverse class.

To find these resources, reach out to colleagues or do research online. Attend conferences or workshops related to language teaching and build connections with other teachers who may have valuable resources to share. You can join online communities or forums where language teachers exchange ideas and resources. Additionally, seek guidance from your school or district to see what resources may already be available for you to use.

STEP 3: Apply the Plan-Do-Study-Act cycle.

Once you have taken inventory of the linguistic diversity in your class and have found resources to help build your capacity as a language teacher, it's time to put this knowledge into action. An effective way to do this is by following the Plan-Do-Study-Act (PDSA) cycle. It involves planning and implementing small changes in your teaching approach based on your research and desired outcomes, observing and studying the results of these changes, and then making necessary adjustments before repeating the cycle.

The PDSA cycle is a systematic series of steps for continuous improvement and learning. It includes these stages:

- *Plan stage:* Identify a goal or purpose, formulate a theory, and define success metrics. This stage can include devising a new teaching technique or integrating a new resource into your curriculum.

- *Do phase:* Execute the plan, make the changes, and collect data for evaluation. This stage might involve introducing a new teaching method in a lesson and observing how it impacts student engagement and understanding.

- *Study phase:* Analyze the data collected in the Do phase and compare the outcomes against your expectations. This work could reflect on whether the new teaching method was effective in improving student comprehension or if it needs adjustments.

- *Act phase:* Reflect on the lessons learned from the entire process and decide on the next steps. This phase could involve refining the teaching method based on the outcomes and feedback or trying a different approach. The cycle then repeats, making the PDSA a dynamic, iterative process that champions continuous improvement and learning.

OVERCOMING PUSHBACK

Communication includes speaking, listening, reading, and writing. Our students cannot afford to miss the skills considered in this Hack. Even our English-only speakers can strive for a better command of the language. Linguistic skills are not one more task to add to your teaching, but they are part of the topics and skills you're teaching. You may receive the following types of pushback, but you can overcome them.

All my students speak English, so I don't need to incorporate language learning strategies. Some educators may question the need to implement language learning strategies when their students already speak English. However, when students are exposed to new languages, it enhances their cognitive skills, broadens their cultural understanding, strengthens their communication skills, and prepares them for more educational and career opportunities. In addition, students who are adept at social English can mask their need for academic support. Social English and academic English are two different skill sets. While students may be comfortable with everyday conversations, they may struggle with academic language, which is more formal and specific. This skill gap can pose a significant barrier to their academic progress. Therefore, it's critical to incorporate language learning strategies, even for students already conversant in social English. This practice boosts their academic language skills and equips them with the tools they need to succeed in a rigorous academic environment.

I cannot take on anything else when my students are already behind. Implementing new strategies and approaches can be overwhelming, especially for educators who feel they are already struggling to keep up with their curriculum. However, incorporating language learning into content areas does not have to be a burden or add extra work. By using existing content and materials, educators can seamlessly integrate language learning into their lessons. This approach benefits all students, not just ELLs, by enhancing overall academic language skills.

Proactively addressing language acquisition can lighten teachers' loads in the long run by equipping students with the linguistic tools they need to understand and engage with the curriculum more effectively. This work can significantly reduce the need for interventions down the line. Students confident in their academic language abilities are less likely to fall behind, reducing the need for catch-up sessions or remedial instruction. In essence, by investing in language support early on, you're facilitating smoother and more efficient learning experiences for your students in the future.

HACK IN ACTION

The story of Ms. Johnson (a pseudonym) is one of a monolingual teacher who rose to meet the needs of her linguistically diverse classroom. She was a colleague of Lissette Jacobson.

Ms. Johnson was a fifth-grade teacher at a diverse school where students came from various cultural and language backgrounds. Her colleagues and leaders admired her classroom management. When you walked into her room, you noticed that the students appeared so engaged that you could hear a pin drop. She strived to create an inclusive and welcoming environment, but she saw that some students struggled to keep up with the material due to linguistic barriers. After doing some research, Ms. Johnson learned about language objectives and how they can improve student understanding and participation. She implemented this Hack in her lesson planning, and the results were astounding.

The first step Ms. Johnson took was to identify the specific language objectives for each lesson, which involved looking at the content standards and determining what language skills students would need to understand and participate in the lesson success-fully. The content standard was on writing a persuasive essay, and the language standard was "Students will be able to use persuasive language to support their arguments." By identifying these objectives, Ms. Johnson was able to have a clear focus on language in her lesson planning.

Once she identified the language objectives, Ms. Johnson incorporated them into her lesson plans, which involved explicitly stating the language objectives at the beginning of each lesson and ensuring they aligned with the content standards. Additionally, she included activities to help students practice and develop their language skills. For example, for the persuasive essay lesson, Ms. Johnson included a mini-lesson on persuasive language and had students work in groups to practice using it in their writing. This experience helped students understand the content and develop their language skills.

THE ROOT OF ALL TEACHING AND LEARNING IS COMMUNICATION. THE ROOT OF COMMUNICATION IS UNDERSTANDING.

In addition to incorporating language objectives into her lesson plans, Ms. Johnson provided language support for her students, such as using visuals and graphic organizers to help clarify information, providing sentence stems and vocabulary lists for writing assignments, and encouraging peer collaboration for speaking activities. By doing this, Ms. Johnson ensured that all students had access to the material regardless of their language background. What was once a quiet classroom soon became a room filled with the sounds of learning and academic discourse.

Finally, Ms. Johnson assessed the language objectives in her lesson evaluation, which involved assessing students' understanding of the content and their language skills. By doing this, she could track students' progress and see how well they met the language objectives.

By implementing language objectives in her lesson planning, Ms. Johnson saw a significant improvement in student understanding and participation. Students who were once struggling due to language were now actively participating and showing a better understanding of the material. Additionally, students' language skills improved over time as they continued to practice and develop them through various activities incorporating the four language domains.

While we have discussed how communication includes more than what we say, we understand that language is a foundational part of how we connect with each another. Our students need us as educators to use precise language that will help support and empower them to thrive. We must ACT to center language in our classrooms.

Actions:

- Check your content for linguistic complexity. Some lessons will include little to no new vocabulary. Other lessons, especially at the beginning of units, include many new words and concepts. This practice pushes beyond vocabulary because some concepts require specific, creative descriptions for students to understand them.

- Learn about your students' language skills, such as their reading levels, understanding of vocabulary, or writing skills. This information will help you scaffold your lessons in ways that support increased student engagement and academic performance.

Consider:

- Many schools and classrooms have students with varying linguistic skill levels. How will you support students with limited English proficiency or students with special needs? How will you challenge students with strong language skills who may be ready for more?

- Language can be a barrier to students doing well on assessments. What words or phrases do students need to know to comprehend what an assessment is asking them to do? How can students be set up for success on state assessments that may use a different language from a given curriculum?

Turning Point:

- The root of all teaching and learning is communication. The root of communication is understanding. It is not sufficient to simply say that a lesson was taught. A check for understanding holds the key to learning. Thinking about language will reduce the number of times a lesson must be retaught due to a lack of comprehension.

CONCLUSION
Leverage Language in All Learning

*If you talk to a man in a language he understands,
that goes to his head. If you talk to him in his
own language, that goes to his heart.*
— NELSON MANDELA, CIVIL RIGHTS ACTIVIST,
FIRST PRESIDENT OF SOUTH AFRICA

E BEGAN THIS book by expounding upon our personal stories and how language has impacted each of our journeys as students and now as education professionals. We hope you walk away from this book with a clearer understanding of how language is present in every classroom and lesson and is an invaluable tool for success in schools across the United States and around the world.

You have reached the conclusion. You have read all the Hacks. You are ready to engage all your students through the leveraging of language. From understanding and instructing your students in the basics of language to reminding them that we are all "language learners," your classrooms and schools are ready to be transformed by implementing the Hacks you have read here. You are prepared to build stronger relationships with your students, their families, and the community, centering language as a key component of our students' identities.

We are all language teachers. The task of teaching our students the art of using language to learn and communicate their learning is not only the role of reading teachers but of all of us who are a part of the education system. We can help produce a more equitable world by elevating the status of all languages. In doing so, we are creating a culture of respect and rapport in which students and staff can learn from each other. This type of culture is our goal.

ABOUT THE AUTHORS

LISSETTE JACOBSON

Lissette Jacobson has dedicated her career to multilingual learners, having worked with culturally and linguistically diverse students in grades K–8. She brings both classroom and administrative experience to this role. She has provided professional development in multi-tiered system of supports (MTSS), curriculum mapping, standards-based instruction, and differentiation.

Lissette's passion for education stems from her experience as a first-generation Mexican American in the public school system. She also serves as an advisory board member of the TEACH Plus Illinois Affinity Group Network. Lissette co-founded Culture, Identity, and Multilingual Advocacy (CIMA), an educational consulting company that addresses current educational challenges through a linguistically and culturally responsive lens. It is crucial for her to affirm her students' identities and elevate the status of the Spanish language.

She married her college sweetheart, Brett, and has two sons, Maxwell and Miguel.

MAURICE McDAVID

Maurice McDavid has a wide array of experience in education. He has taught middle school history and Spanish, as well as high school world geography. Maurice moved into administration as a dean at a high school sixty miles west of Chicago. He now serves as principal of a dual language elementary school in the western suburbs.

While social justice and restorative justice have always been driving factors in his work, his interest in early literacy and linguistics has grown during his current tenure. He has offered professional development in all those areas in various settings. He also served on the Illinois Diverse and Learner Ready Teacher Network and helped to author the Culturally Responsive Teaching and Leading (CRTL) standards.

Maurice is married to his high school sweetheart, Samantha, and has three children, Ezekiel, Cinderella, and Zariah.

TOGETHER

Together, Lissette Jacobson and Maurice McDavid co-founded Black, Brown & Bilingüe, a podcast dedicated to creating a world in which Black and Brown identities are affirmed, multilingualism and multiculturalism are nurtured, and equity is at the center of all conversations.

Connect with the Authors
website: BlackBrownBilingue.com
email: blackbrownbilingue@gmail.com
X (Twitter): @blkbrwnbilingue
LinkedIn: Lissette Jacobson and Maurice McDavid

ACKNOWLEDGMENTS

LISSETTE JACOBSON

First and foremost, I would like to extend my deepest gratitude to my husband, Brett, for his unwavering support throughout this journey called life. Your love, patience, and encouragement have been my pillars of strength. Thank you for always believing in me and pushing me to reach for my dreams.

My two sons, Maxwell and Miguel, have been a constant source of inspiration. Your presence brings joy and meaning into my life. I am grateful for your love, laughter, and endless hugs that keep me going even on the toughest days. No accomplishment or milestone can top the privilege of being your mom. You are the definition of pride and joy. Mommy loves you endlessly.

To my parents for their courage and hard work throughout their lives. You have been the best example to me as an educator, wife, mother, and human being. *Los quiero con todo mi corazón.*

To my siblings, Lorena, Miguel, Jose, and Daisy, for shaping me into who I am today. Even with the good, bad, and the ugly, our family is one I wouldn't trade for the world. Daisy, you're my soulmate. Thanks for being an amazing sister and even more amazing auntie to my boys.

To my mentors, both formal and informal, I am deeply grateful for your invaluable insights, advice, and guidance. You have steered me through the various stages of life, shedding light on the path when the way forward was unclear. Your faith in my abilities has been a source of strength and motivation. Thank you for your tireless efforts in helping me become better at my craft. You have become some of my closest friends. Thank you, Maurice McDavid, Tom Kim, Billy Hueramo, and Amonaquenette Parker. To James Cohen and Jan Woodhouse—the best professors at Northern Illinois University.

To my students, both current and former, thank you for teaching me just as much, if not more, than I taught you. You have enriched my life with your enthusiasm, curiosity, and resilience, inspiring me every day to be the best educator I can be. Your growth and accomplishments are my greatest rewards. I am so proud of each of you. Special thanks to my angels in room 7. You brought joy in the darkest of times.

Thank you, God, for everything in my life.

MAURICE McDAVID

I give thanks to God, above all else, for the opportunity I have had to serve in the field of education. It has been the foundation of all that is in this book.

Thank you to my family, my mother, my wife, and my children. They have been my incredible supporters in this writing process, giving me the time I needed to produce this work.

Although it may go without saying, I want to say it. I am so grateful to have an awesome friend and thought partner to coauthor this book. Thank you, Lissette, for the many thought-provoking conversations and the times you have challenged me to be a better educator. A final thank-you to every colleague who has added some word of wisdom or instruction to my life and career. It has paid dividends in this book, which I hope is our first of many.

SNEAK PEEK

5

BUILD ON STUDENT STRENGTHS
From What's Wrong to What's Strong

Well-being should be taught in school because it would be an antidote to the runaway incidence of depression, a way to increase life satisfaction, and an aid to better learning and more creative thinking.

— MARTIN SELIGMAN, FOUNDER OF POSITIVE PSYCHOLOGY

THE BELIEF:
WE SHOULD ONLY FOCUS ON ADDRESSING STUDENT DEFICIENCIES

WE RECENTLY HELD a workshop to help educators name, know, and use their strengths. We asked the audience to raise their hands if they could readily name their top five strengths. Out of about 250 participants, only about fifteen people raised their hands. We then asked how many people could name two or three of their top strengths. This time, about ten to fifteen more hands went up. Then, we asked how many people could name at least a single strength they might have. Still, only a few more hands went up.

In this exercise, the intent is to see how many people can readily name their top strengths. Like clockwork, regardless of the city, location, or demographic, few people can readily name their strengths. But why? Why do people have such a hard time identifying and naming their top strengths?

For starters, it's hard for people to speak affirmatively about themselves. Sadly, they have been conditioned or taught that their weaknesses define them. As a result, they view and maneuver the world through a deficit lens. Another reason people struggle is that it's much easier to name our weaknesses and deficits. This difficulty isn't exclusive to adults either.

As practitioners inside schools, we have found that students across age and grade levels struggle to identify and name their strengths. It's not surprising that a room full of 250 adults struggled to name their strengths. They once were children who, most likely, were never required to readily name, know, and use their strengths. Our responsibility as educators is to help students leverage their assets in a way that no one taught us.

THE REFRAME:
BUILD UP STUDENT STRENGTHS

Students need to be able to name, know, and use their strengths. Educators can be much more intentional about helping students build their strengths, not just prioritizing their weaknesses and what they can't do. School administrators, mental health personnel, teachers, and other school-based staff must commit to using a strength-based approach to help students actively develop their strengths.

Benefits of a strength-based approach to building up students

The strength-based approach focuses on a person's unique strengths, assets, and capabilities. It is a philosophy that sees people as resourceful, resilient, and capable of change. This approach empowers people to take control of their lives and create positive outcomes for themselves.

We emphasize the key belief that every person has many strengths and abilities they use when facing challenges. We offer a solution-focused perspective with clients to identify their strengths and utilize them to overcome problems in their lives.

The strength-based approach values building off what works rather than focusing on what doesn't. It promotes a positive view of the individual and encourages connecting with one's social supports like family or community to spur on their transformation.

We must promote individual well-being. It's holistic and human-centered because it sees the humanity in people. In the context of schools, using a strength-based approach allows every student the potential to thrive. Students not only learn to understand their strengths within this system, but they also use them in the context of their lives and communities. The motivation is simple: it works. Research shows that when students understand their strengths and use them to gain skills and increase productivity, they experience stronger self-confidence, greater academic success, and better relationships with peers, teachers, and parents.

> When we encourage children to identify, explore, and use their strengths, they gain the confidence to develop skills in other areas.

Many young people experience feelings of inadequacy and self-doubt as they try to thrive in a world that doesn't always see their gifts and talents as important. By encouraging students to understand their innate skills and abilities, you can help them remember how exceptional they are.

As an educator (or parent), to help students develop their strengths, place value on what's working over what's not working. To help people find value in what's working, ask questions like:

- What makes you feel happy?

- What draws people to you?

- What activities are easy for you?

- What do you consider to be your greatest strengths?

- Describe a time when things went well for you. Why did they go well?

When a child understands their strengths, it equips them to make better choices about how to spend their time—and how to shape their lives. When we encourage children to identify, explore, and use their strengths, they gain the confidence to develop skills in other areas. Research from the University of Pennsylvania and the field of Positive Psychology demonstrates that helping students build their strengths promotes academic achievement, happiness, and a sense of self-efficacy. It supports student well-being.

Perhaps the most important aspect of helping students develop strengths is teaching them how to be solution-focused. This can be difficult for students because it involves teaching them to focus on what worked in the past and what works now, even when facing insurmountable problems or obstacles.

One effective way to teach this skill is to have students keep a journal to write down each day's successes. You can do this as a class, small group, or at the individual level. Everyone can share something they've done well or accomplished that day. You can also create a class journal where each student contributes one entry per week. Parents or caregivers can do this at home too.

One of our favorite activities helps students build their strengths by noticing and reflecting on what went well. The activity is called Three Good Things. Dr. Martin Seligman and his team at the University of Pennsylvania studied and researched this activity, which increases happiness and decreases depressive symptoms for six months. Participants in the Three Good Things exercise showed beneficial effects one month following the test.

At the one-month follow-up, participants were happier and less depressed than they had been at the baseline, and they stayed happier and less depressed at the three-month and six-month follow-ups.

This is a powerful exercise because it shifts your focus from things that were wrong to things that were strong. This positive mindset can improve your overall well-being and lift your mood. The Three Good Things exercise helps students reflect on themselves—*and* why they were good. See Image 5.1.

Try this exercise with your students or loved ones at home:

1. At the end of each day, write down Three Good Things that happened that day.

2. Write *why* each thing went well.

3. Do this for at least a week straight.

Image 5.1: The Three Good Things activity.

WHAT YOU CAN DO TOMORROW

By taking a strength-based approach to education, you can help your students develop their skills and talents to realize their full potential. Let's help kids figure out what they're good at and improve those areas. Let's prioritize helping students build their strengths and practice using them daily. That will help them feel happier, experience more flow, and keep doing activities they enjoy—even when they have to do other activities they don't like. Educators and even parents who use a strength-based approach will help children become more invested in their learning and more engaged in the classroom.

The SPOT process can help students develop their strengths. It stands for Strength observation; Progress over perfection; Opportunity to shine; and Teach, try, and tap into strengths.

Strength observation. A strength observation is a way to proactively search for strengths in your students. Try immersing yourself in their environment, such as the classroom, hallway, cafeteria, and after-school events. A strength observation differs from a traditional observation because you are intentionally searching for the positive. As a strength observer, it's not your job to be right but to learn more about who you observe. That requires being open and receptive to what you may or may not see.

What is the most important trait in a strength observer? Curiosity! You need to understand your students' behaviors, experiences, and desires. You'll need to ask questions that you might think are obvious or irrelevant. The more time you spend with them, the more you learn about their strengths. One of the most important steps to becoming a strength observer is adopting an explorer's mindset. This means that you approach the observation with an open mind—without any preconceived notions—and seek to discover various strengths. It also means being open to every possibility. When you immerse yourself in your students' worlds, you give yourself permission to be curious and wonder. Then you open yourself to discovering new strengths within your students.

In a successful strength observation, you will ask questions, expect unconventional answers, and learn about the students' worlds. Searching for strengths in your students might seem intuitive, but it's not. Since most of us, as educators, were trained to identify students' deficits, we have to actively work to identify their strengths. Pay attention to the following:

- Does the student work better independently or in a group?
- When does the student show excitement, boredom, more energy or less energy, frustration, or sustained focus?
- How easily do they initiate tasks, shift between tasks, and stay on task?
- Are they inspiring or motivating others?
- Are they creative in how they approach a given task?
- Do they leverage resources or social capital in a meaningful way?

- What was challenging for the student?
- What seemed easy for the student?
- What patterns did you notice throughout the observation?

After the observation, review your findings with the student. Specifically, share the strengths you identified. For example, if you observed a student during math class while they had to sustain attention over a long period of time, you might say, "Your attention to detail is strong, and you were able to focus on the entire task to get the job done." Maybe you observed a student who didn't contribute much during the brainstorming portion of the group activity in social studies. Still, that student captivated his peers and had them on the edge of their seats during the group presentation to the whole class.

Next, have the student offer their reflections on how they view their strengths. Ask them if they agree with your assessment. This is an opportunity to get feedback on how well your observations match up with how the students see themselves—and it also helps students learn more about themselves!

To take this a step further, help students reflect on their strengths by asking questions like:

- What do you think you are good at?
- What do you love to do?
- What comes easily to you?
- Are there any activities that make you lose track of time?

Progress over perfection. Identifying and using strengths can be hard because most of us aren't used to tapping into our strengths. The key here is to help young people understand the importance of progress. The reality is that routinely using your strengths is a skill. LeBron James is arguably the greatest basketball player of our generation, and he practices his craft daily.

We can also practice our strength-finding skills every day. Some days will be more challenging than others. Make progress toward the goal, not perfection. Help your students find new ways to use their strengths and get better every day.

Opportunity to shine. When students use their strengths, it gives them a chance to shine, and they are more likely to experience success. This builds self-efficacy and gives them a reason to persist, even when tasks are challenging.

Simply put, when students have an opportunity to use their strengths and shine, they experience positive emotions and feel good about themselves.

Imagine a child with perseverance as a strength who only has one shot at succeeding at a task. If they aren't successful on the first try, that child might become frustrated and learn that you have to be perfect, contributing to anxiety. Imagine if a student has a signature strength of perseverance, and you give them multiple chances to demonstrate mastery. The student might not succeed on the first try, the second try, or even the third. But providing a student who demonstrates perseverance with the opportunity to work at the task until they are successful will help them feel accomplished and continue to work at it even when they face adversity.

Creating opportunities for students to use and demonstrate their strengths is an excellent way to build self-confidence. Students will begin to believe in themselves, realize they are capable, and leverage their strengths in meaningful ways. Also, there is value in helping students recognize and identify missed opportunities for using their strengths. The idea here is that if students can identify these missed opportunities, then it might help to increase their awareness of future opportunities to use strengths.

Teach, try, and tap into strengths. Teach students to explicitly name their strengths. Help them to build up their strength-based vocabulary, and show them the power of "yet." Instead of a student saying they are not good at math facts, please encourage them to say, "I might not be the best in math facts–*YET*." Encourage young people to *try* their strengths in new ways. If their strength is "focus," ask them to try a new task like finding a solution to a problem no one has figured out yet.

Help your students find ways to tap into the strengths of others. Why? Because the best schools, communities, teams, and organizations know how to harness the strengths of each other–and you can help your students do the same.

This means helping students become well-attuned to their strengths and limitations and learn how to work with others with different strengths and limitations.

For example, some people are fantastic at making decisions quickly and effectively. Others are great at seeing all possible consequences of a decision. Some find inspiration in unexpected places. When you have a team that is familiar with each individual's approach, you can create a culture where everyone feels comfortable contributing to what they're best at. This leads to bigger and better ideas than if everyone just worked on their own, and it also leads to increased trust in the team—which is what makes them stronger overall.

One way to help people tap into the strengths of others is to ask them, "How might you use one of your strengths to help someone else?"

BUY
HACKING DEFICIT THINKING

AVAILABLE AT:
10publications.com
Amazon.com
and bookstores near you

MORE FROM
TIMES 10 PUBLICATIONS

Hacking School Discipline
9 Ways to Create a Culture of Empathy & Responsibility Using Restorative Justice
By Nathan Maynard and Brad Weinstein

Reviewers proclaim this *Washington Post* Bestseller as "maybe the most important book a teacher can read, a must for all educators, fabulous, a game changer!" Learn how to eliminate punishment and build a culture of responsible students and independent learners. Twenty-one straight months at #1 on Amazon, *Hacking School Discipline* is disrupting education like nothing we've seen in decades—maybe centuries.

Hacking School Discipline TOGETHER
10 Ways to Create a Culture of Empathy and Responsibility Using Schoolwide Restorative Justice

By Jeffrey Benson

This sequel to *Hacking School Discipline* is for teachers, administrators, and staff who long to create a school that fosters responsibility, forgiveness, and accountability so students learn from their impulsive decisions. We can change the status quo in which students believe their biggest mistake was getting caught. Instead, learn how to create a school where administrators and staff trust each other, and students benefit from what we do best: educate.

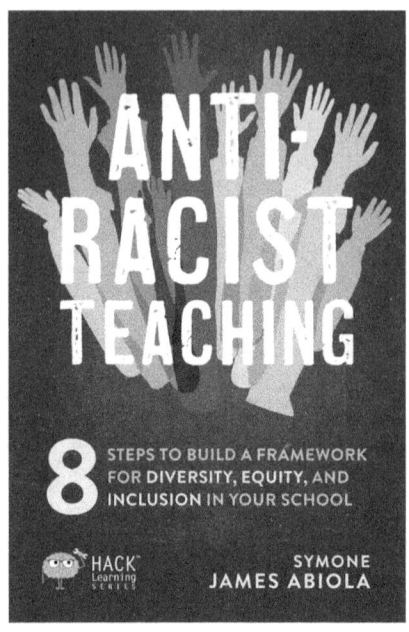

Anti-Racist Teaching
8 Steps to Build a Framework for Diversity, Equity, and Inclusion in Your School

By Symone James Abiola

Believing that racism is wrong is not enough; we must take action to address racial inequities within schools. As educators, engaging in the foundational work of addressing racial inequity and uplifting all students is our highest responsibility to the students and families we serve. Use this guide to actively address the impact of racism and bias in your school and provide an empowering educational experience for all students.

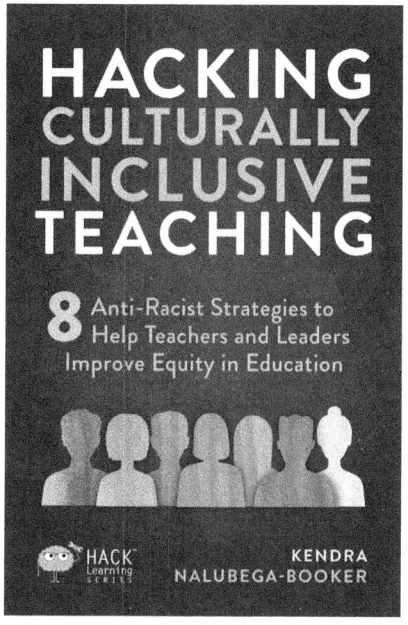

Hacking Culturally Inclusive Teaching
8 Anti-Racist Strategies That Help Teachers and Leaders Improve Equity in Education
By Kendra Nalubega-Booker

Culturally and linguistically diverse students often lack representation and inclusion in the classroom, hindering their academic success. Yet when teachers integrate culturally sustaining practices, they help all students understand our global community and situate themselves within it. Education leader Kendra Nalubega-Booker shows step-by-step strategies and best practices that shine a light on our students' rich languages and cultures and create equitable learning for all.

Learning Lifeguards
Your 10-Step Guide to Building a Team That Motivates Struggling Students to Love Learning and Stay in School
By Sherri Nelson

Many students grapple with academic riptides, desperately trying to stay afloat. As educators, do we turn away, or do we pool our resources and skills to prevent them from drowning? This empowering guide equips educators with actionable strategies for creating a school community where every student succeeds. Whether you're a teacher seeking solutions or a visionary principal, you can be an academic lifeline for your students.

Preventing Polarization
50 Strategies for Teaching Kids about Empathy, Politics, and Civic Responsibility
By Michelle Blanchet and Brian Deters

In an era that has become incredibly polarized politically and socially, we can help our students learn to come together despite differences and become active and engaged citizens. A one-off civics course is not enough. Learn essential strategies to create experiences that help students break down barriers through activities and role-playing. Let's show our students how to make a difference, minimize conflict, and build accord.

GET THE EDGE NOW

Teaching and leading is harder than ever … so Times 10 Publications created *Educator's Edge*, free weekly content with classroom-tested Hacks, leadership insights, inclusive teaching strategies, and simple solutions to complex challenges. Join a growing community of teachers and leaders who are finding smarter, faster ways to teach, lead, and grow.

Sign up now at **10publications.com/educators-edge**.

TIMES 10 PUBLICATIONS provides practical solutions that busy people can read today and use tomorrow. We bring you content from experienced researchers and practitioners, and we share it through books, podcasts, webinars, articles, events, and ongoing conversations on social media. Our books and materials help turn practice into action. Stay in touch with us at HackLearningLife.com and 10Publications.com and follow our updates @10Publications.

www.ingramcontent.com/pod-product-compliance
Lightning Source LLC
Chambersburg PA
CBHW061144120626
46546CB00005B/1920